Instant Gratitude

365 Days of Grace, Ease, and Laughter

Copyright © 2018 Ilana Kristeva. All rights reserved.

This publication may not be reproduced or transmitted in any form, part or whole, manually or digitally, including photocopying, scanning, audio recording, videotaping, or otherwise, without prior written consent from the author.

Limit of Liability: All contents of this publication were prepared for inspirational and entertainment purposes only. It contains general information about health, nutrition, relationships, and time management practices but offers no medical or financial advice. The tools, techniques, and processes described serve as the author's testimonial of their effectiveness, not commercial endorsements for any product or service. The author shall not be held liable for any results, or lack thereof, with regard to medical conditions, financial loss or profit, or any other outcomes. Readers must use their own discretion regarding any suggestion or strategy contained herein and should never delay seeking professional help for their medical, relationship, or financial issues.

INSTANT GRATITUDE: 365 DAYS OF GRACE, EASE, AND LAUGHTER

INSTANT GRATITUDE COLLECTION, VOLUME 1

By Ilana Kristeva

Paperback ISBN: 978-0-9963037-4-3
Electronic Book Text: ISBN: 978-0-9963037-5-0
Digital (format EPUB): ISBN: 978-0-9963037-3-6
Audio Book ISBN: 978-0-9963037-8-1

Book Cover Design: Debbie O'Byrne at JETLAUNCH.net
Book Design: JETLAUNCH.net
Compilation Editor: Giovanni Dortch
Back Cover Author Photo: Hope Harris at hopeimages.com

Field of Choices
www.fieldofchoices.com

Other books written and narrated by Ilana Kristeva:

Birth of a Self-Care Vigilante, Tap into the Universe for Recovery, Book 1 (paperback and eBook)

Audio Book for *Birth of a Self-Care Vigilante, Tap into the Universe for Recovery, Book 1* (available Summer 2018)

To all my adult friends who embrace the kid *within* while seeking new adventures. May we live our *best lives ever* at this very moment!

Table of Contents

Introduction ix

Gratitude Expressions

January. 1

February 32

March 61

April 92

May..................................122

June 152

July 182

August 213

September 244

October 274

November 305

December 335

Bonus Gratitude Expressions 366

Index 375

Acknowledgements 377

About Ilana Kristeva 379

Introduction

I was the Queen of Self-Abandonment, now known as the Self-Care Vigilante. Although still very gifted in making excuses and complaining about anything under the sun, a well-mastered art form of mine, I feel that this fun and sexy pastime is overrated. Every morning, I make a commitment to set aside my tiara and stay off my platinum-plated pity pot. *Ahh!* Fresh air is wonderful.

Now I know what it is like to be *in love with life.* The noise pollution in my brain that made me feel very old has dissipated. A deeply grounded sense of victory feeds the dancing inner flame of my soul. Throughout the day, I bathe in blessings of grace, ease, and laughter no matter what happens. Would you like to join me?

Let's transform our yuckies into yummies to feel more fantastic in our bodies. We can quickly dissolve the onslaught of floods, fires, and hurricanes of negative thinking in the brain between our ears. Facing injuries, illness, and isolation with a changed attitude, we thrive on sparks of creativity and splashes of laughter every single day no matter how the world may appear.

I challenge you to transform what you perceive as *awful* into something *awesome.* The Universe flows; we block. Let's get out of our own way now by looking for things to be grateful for throughout the day while letting go of disappointment, fear, anger, self-pity, grief, and shame. We aim to flow: *F.L.O.W.—Feel Light Offering Wisdom* (from *Birth of a Self-Care Vigilante,* p. 123). Yes!

Note that I am a realist; life *will* always send us challenges. With an attitude of gratitude, however, we can turn things around *in an instant.* Use *Instant Gratitude* to jumpstart your brain and your spirit! With daily doses of meditation—for physical, mental, and spiritual vitality, higher vibrational frequencies of joy, compassion, and love are within your reach.

Here are 365 of my 1,500+ daily gratitude

blasts for you to enjoy, share, and laugh with others. Living with chronic pain, depression, compulsions, and other serious conditions has propelled me to bask in gratitude. My favorite topics include:

- Self-care of body, mind, and spirit
- Healthy boundaries
- Intestinal health and gut intuition
- Nutrition for robust immune systems
- Neuroplasticity and retraining the brain
- Emotional Freedom Technique (EFT) or meridian "tapping"
- Prosperity and abundance consciousness
- Positive visibility through physical and spiritual fitness
- Universe, Source, or Higher Power
- Emotional sobriety and serenity

Writing expressions of gratitude is a special brand of practical spirituality that has truly made a difference in the quality of my time here on Earth. It is my hope that you, too, will *fall in love with life* during your visit. Together, we dissolve remaining traces of bitterness and cultivate our inner gardens to serve the Universe from a place of plenty!

Ilana Kristeva
Self-Care Vigilante
Founder of Field of Choices

Instant Gratitude

January 1

I am grateful for so many things on the outside; however, feeling comfortable in my own body—right here, right now—is most precious. I would rather be me than anyone else. Happy New Year from my insides to your insides!

❖

Dear Reader: What part of your body, inside or out, could use some extra attention and tender loving care (TLC) at this very moment? Let's send good thoughts and warmth to it right now.

My thoughts:

_____
_____
_____
_____
_____

Additional key words: PROSPERITY and ABUNDANCE / SELF-WORTH

January 2

I am grateful that by carrying beautiful places and people in my heart, I can live, work, and thrive anywhere the Universe truly needs me.

My thoughts:

_____
_____
_____
_____
_____

Additional key words: SERENITY / PURPOSE

Instant Gratitude

January 3

I am grateful the Universe sends me thoughtful, kind, and creative friends and strangers. Perhaps this emerges from the way I treat the world, too.

My thoughts:

_____
_____
_____
_____
_____

Additional key words: SUPPORT TEAM

January 4

I am grateful that whenever I feel overwhelmed, I immediately ask my internal organs what minerals and vitamins they may need.

❁

Dear Reader: Can you offer your body fresh or lightly steamed vegetables today? Let's explore the many rich nutrients that veggies offer our bodies.

My thoughts:

_____
_____
_____
_____
_____

Additional key words: FOOD and NUTRIENTS

Instant Gratitude

January 5

I am grateful for easy-to-prepare remedies for strengthening my teeth and gums; consistent mouth care is great for the immune system. Thank goodness for oil pulling, salt-water rising, and apple cider vinegar-ing!

My thoughts:

_____
_____
_____
_____
_____

Additional key words: BODY CARE

January 6

I am grateful to witness the transformation in people who are leaving behind old habits and toxic resentments. What an honor it is to witness their *evolving new stories*.

My thoughts:

Additional key words: VICTORY and CELEBRATION

January 7

I am grateful for bookending. Telling someone what I am going to do, doing it, and then saying that it's done makes me feel incredible! It moves me forward in serving others with integrity.

My thoughts:

_____
_____
_____
_____
_____

Additional key words: SPIRIT and SOUL / WORK

January 8

I am grateful that I hand over my fear and worry to Source, Great Spirit, Sweetness, Creator, or God, so I may move forward feeling light, creative, and free!

My thoughts:

_____
_____
_____
_____
_____

Additional key words: HIGHER POWER and UNIVERSE

Instant Gratitude

January 9

I am grateful for the *guts* to face my shame and guilt and discharge the toxins from my body's cells. Feeling clean from the inside out is fabulous!

My thoughts:

_____
_____
_____
_____
_____

Additional key words: BODY CARE

January 10

I am grateful to know that I naturally complicate just about everything. Acknowledging this is self-empowering. My mantra: UNcomplicate. Period.

My thoughts:

_____
_____
_____
_____
_____

Additional key words: MINDSET / SELF-WORTH

Instant Gratitude

January 11

I am grateful for sunny mornings. They are proof that there is a God, Source, Great Spirit—a magnificent source of energy beyond myself that is turning Earth on its axis while I sleep!

My thoughts:

_____
_____
_____
_____
_____

Additional key words: NATURE and WEATHER / HIGHER POWER and UNIVERSE

January 12

I am grateful for my expanding belief that resources are limitless. Adjusting my lenses enables me to see a broader field of choices and allows the Universe to guide me.

My thoughts:

_____
_____
_____
_____

Additional key words: MINDSET / HIGHER POWER and UNIVERSE / PROSPERITY and ABUNDANCE

Instant Gratitude

January 13

I am grateful for the guts to be blunt when appropriate. My life on Earth is a blink of an eye; I choose to live it with courage and purpose.

❈

Dear Reader: Can you think of one area in which you would like greater courage to speak your truth? Let's take deep breaths throughout the day and allow divine guidance to support us.

My thoughts:

_____
_____
_____
_____
_____

Additional key words: COURAGE and ACTION

January 14

I am grateful for my commitment to trying new exercises that improve blood flow, maintain balance, and increase strength. Consistent self-care evidently goes a *long* way.

My thoughts:

_____
_____
_____
_____
_____

Additional key words: BODY CARE

Instant Gratitude

January 15

I am grateful for deep breathing-and-stretching meditations, time tracking, and other mindfulness tools. Having clarity minimizes wreckage that comes with falling into a rabbit hole of unsatisfying fantasies.

My thoughts:

_____
_____
_____
_____
_____

Additional key words: TIME / PRAYER and MEDITATION

January 18

I am grateful that whenever I find the world to be harsh or irritating, it is an occasion to turn inward and become a gentler and more compassionate person to *myself and others*. Delicious!

My thoughts:

_____

_____

_____

_____

_____

Additional key words: SPIRIT and SOUL

Instant Gratitude

January 19

I am grateful for the kid in me who remembers to focus on fun and joy in each of my grown-up tasks. Getting honest about my motives behind the never-ending "to do" list liberates me.

My thoughts:

_____
_____
_____
_____
_____

Additional key words: CHILD-LIKE JOY

January 20

I am grateful my imagination can take me to awesome places. Resting in my bed under a roof, I went camping last night. The cool breeze was fantastic and the night sky so intriguing. And when morning arrived she kissed my face with her sunshine!

My thoughts:

_____
_____
_____
_____
_____

Additional key words: INSPIRATION and CREATIVITY / NATURE and WEATHER

Instant Gratitude

January 21

I am grateful for willingness to acknowledge my many accomplishments and victories, but they are truly my Creator's successes!

My thoughts:

_____
_____
_____
_____
_____

Additional key words: VICTORY and CELEBRATION / HIGHER POWER and UNIVERSE

January 22

I am grateful that I love going to the gym, *not* because I am afraid of needing a wheelchair again but because athletes inspire me to stay connected to my body and reach new heights.

My thoughts:

_____
_____
_____
_____
_____

Additional key words: SPORTS and ATHLETICS / BODY CARE

Instant Gratitude

January 23

I am grateful for all the stability and consistency that my Creator and I have woven into my life, especially the art of daily self-care. My physical and spiritual fitness grants me access to unexpected adventures that stretch me and expand my world.

My thoughts:

_____
_____
_____
_____
_____

Additional key words: BODY CARE / SPIRIT and SOUL / HIGHER POWER and UNIVERSE

January 24

I am grateful for the tools of time tracking and time planning. Getting honest about how long it truly takes me to do something empowers me to design a grounded yet flowing, divine-inspired schedule.

My thoughts:

_____
_____
_____
_____
_____

Additional key words: HIGHER POWER / TIME

Instant Gratitude

January 25

I am grateful for remembering to put one foot in front of the other. And laughing to "pee-point" makes my day even more splendid!*

* "Pee-point" comes from my Self-Care Vigilante Affirmation #3: "I laugh to 'pee-point' every single day" in *Birth of a Self-Care Vigilante*, p.190.

My thoughts:

_____
_____
_____
_____
_____

Additional key words: MINDSET / CHILD-LIKE JOY

January 26

I am grateful for reminders that earning less than what I am worth is self-deprivation. To truly be of service, I must practice self-care. My feeling fantastic brings great energy and higher productivity to the table.

My thoughts:

_____
_____
_____
_____
_____

Additional key words: SELF-WORTH / SELF-CARE / SERVICE

Instant Gratitude

January 27

I am grateful for the courage to write a list of all the ways I have deceived myself into accepting unacceptable behavior. God, grant me the confidence to come out of hiding, so others may have courage to do so as well.

❊

Dear Reader: What is the "something" you feel too embarrassed to talk about with someone? Let's allow the Universe to show us whom to trust and share it with so we can be free of fear, shame, and illness.

My thoughts:

_____
_____
_____
_____
_____

Additional key words: SPIRIT and SOUL

January 28

I am grateful my gut intuition tells me things the brain between my ears does not know or cannot understand.

My thoughts:

_____
_____
_____
_____
_____

Additional key words: WISDOM and INTUITION

Instant Gratitude

January 29

I am grateful for my happy intestines. Taking good care of them leads to more mental clarity and a stronger immune system. We totally win!

My thoughts:

_____
_____
_____
_____
_____

Additional key words: BODY CARE / FOOD and NUTRIENTS

January 30

I am grateful to feel so nourished right now without a craving for anything, except for needing to pee and drink more water—*again*. Is this what it's like to be a cat?

❈

Dear Reader: Have you ever wondered why animals naturally take good care of themselves while humans need instructions to do so? Let's take time to quiet our minds today and learn what we can from our favorite animals.

My thoughts:

_____

_____

_____

_____

_____

Additional key words: SERENITY / SELF-CARE and BODY

Instant Gratitude

January 31

I am grateful for good sleep. It truly brings clarity to the forefront. I love making decisions with confidence!

My thoughts:

_____
_____
_____
_____
_____

Additional key words: SLEEP and REST

February 1

I am grateful for the slogan "This, too, shall pass ... like gas." And, for even greater serenity, I "let go and let God" take care of whatever is not mine, as life is more fun and meaningful when I'm "staying in my hula hoop!"

My thoughts:

_____
_____
_____
_____
_____

Additional key words: HEALTHY BOUNDARIES / SPIRIT and SOUL

February 2

I am grateful to wake up with two arms and two legs that are fully intact and sometimes free of pain. A reminder (or two) that I am not alone in the world helps me to feel sane.

❧

Dear Reader: Do you or someone you know suffer from chronic pain or illness? Let's offer compassion to all who are in pain, as no one really knows what it feels like to be in someone else's body, but we can feel grateful for *what we have and can do.*

My thoughts:

_____
_____
_____
_____
_____

Additional key words: PROSPERITY and ABUNDANCE / BODY / PAIN / SERENITY

February 3

I am grateful for my guts to strive for greater intestinal fitness. My small and large intestines love cruciferous veggies, hot water, gentle stretching, and "tapping" on meridian points to better absorb what my body needs and reject what it does not. With thanks, I salute my poop out the door!

My thoughts:

_____
_____
_____
_____
_____

Additional key words: BODY CARE / FOOD and NUTRIENTS

Instant Gratitude

February 4

I am grateful to be able to choose how I see the world—scary and dangerous or full of beautiful surprises. I'll take the goodies, thank you!

My thoughts:

_____
_____
_____
_____
_____

Additional key words: MINDSET

February 5

I am grateful that despite all the uncertainties in my world, Mother Earth holds me safe in her arms. With a stone in my hand, rock beneath my feet, and loving people around the world, I thrive!

My thoughts:

_____
_____
_____
_____
_____

Additional key words: NATURE / SUPPORT TEAM

Instant Gratitude

February 6

I am grateful that ducks are trained to assist people suffering from Post-Traumatic Stress Disorder (PTSD). Emotional Support Ducks can even enjoy window seats on planes while caring for their patients.

❈

Dear Reader: Might you or someone you know benefit from having an animal, such as a dog or a duck? Let's take action to bring together many more trained animals and people who have mental, emotional, and/or physical challenges.

My thoughts:

_____
_____
_____
_____
_____

Additional key words: PUBLIC HEALTH and SAFETY / SERVICE

February 7

I am grateful to be meeting so many people in their fifties who are growing wise gracefully, like me. Appreciating life—having a blast on this planet—is so incredibly sweet.

My thoughts:

_____
_____
_____
_____
_____

Additional key words: SUPPORT TEAM

February 8

I am grateful to be doing things I have been afraid to do, meeting people I have been afraid to meet, and traveling to places I have been afraid to travel. There are new blessings every which way I turn!

My thoughts:

_____
_____
_____
_____
_____

Additional key words: COURAGE and ACTION

February 9

I am grateful *not* to be coughing, sneezing, and hurting or feeling headachy, fatigued, and stressed. Practicing H.A.L.T. ("Don't get too Hungry, Angry, Lonely, or Tired")* is vital for my health and safety and *yours*.

*This acronym or slogan is used in numerous 12-Step recovery programs.

My thoughts:

___

___

___

___

___

Additional key words: BODY CARE

Instant Gratitude

February 10

I am grateful for life-affirming activities, like bantering with hilarious people, creating new healthy dishes, coaching the Red Sox from the middle of my living room floor, and hiking beautiful trails. My Creator *rocks!*

My thoughts:

_____
_____
_____
_____
_____

Additional key words: FUN and HEALTH / SPORTS and ATHLETICS / HIGHER POWER and UNIVERSE

February 11

I am grateful for the wisdom to know the difference between what I can and cannot change. Social transformation is possible through my personal transformation.

My thoughts:

_____
_____
_____
_____
_____

Additional key words: SPIRIT and SOUL

Instant Gratitude

February 12

I am grateful for subtle yet clear signs of serenity. While going through the day with fresh new eyes, I notice dark clouds, traffic, and glum people, but *nothing* can pop my joy bubbles.

❖

Dear Reader: How would you feel with an invisible energy shield around you that could bounce off what you do not need to absorb? Let's clean up our own thoughts, feelings, and energy today so that positivity comes our way!

My thoughts:

_____
_____
_____
_____
_____

Additional key words: CHILD-LIKE JOY / SPIRIT and SOUL

February 13

I am grateful for my willingness to tap into a Source of wisdom that saves me from overexerting myself. Moderation, balance, and synchronicity *within*—Yay!

My thoughts:

_____
_____
_____
_____
_____

Additional key words: HIGHER POWER and UNIVERSE / BODY CARE

Instant Gratitude

February 14

I am grateful for my newfound awareness that it truly does take courage to love and to be loved. I am responsible for dissolving *exquisite noise pollution* and feeding my heart with vibrant energy!*

* "Exquisite noise pollution" is an expression I use to describe the influx of information into my mind from a variety of sources (professionals, publications, etc.) that is potentially helpful yet inappropriate for my current condition.

My thoughts:

_____
_____
_____
_____
_____

Additional key words: SPIRIT and SOUL / COURAGE and ACTION

February 15

I am grateful for people in my life who are like a great cup of java. *Zing!* Just the thought of them gives me a boost of energy at the gym, self-control in the grocery store, and inspiration to write. Yay for exhilaration *without* caffeine!

❀

Dear Reader: Who in your life gives you an immediate *wow* feeling just by thinking of them? Let's allow more people with that special *zing* into our lives to support us in flowing through the day!

My thoughts:

_____
_____
_____
_____
_____

Additional key words: SUPPORT TEAM / PROSPERITY and ABUNDANCE

Instant Gratitude

February 16

I am grateful for impulse control: healthy food and drink (50%) + EFT tapping (50%) + God (100%) = 200% willingness, footwork, and awesome results!

My thoughts:

_____
_____
_____
_____
_____

Additional key words: SPIRIT and SOUL / HIGHER POWER and UNIVERSE / FOOD and NUTRIENTS

February 17

I am grateful that I eat when I am hungry and sleep when I am tired. A lifestyle of great habits keeps me productive, safe, and a joy to be around.

My thoughts:

_____
_____
_____
_____
_____

Additional key words: BODY CARE / PUBLIC HEALTH and SAFETY

Instant Gratitude

February 18

I am grateful to see that for every event that might "shatter" my life, there is something just as beautiful that could enhance it. Anxiety has had its chance, but it's *off the menu* today!

My thoughts:

_____
_____
_____
_____
_____

Additional key words: SPIRIT and SOUL

February 19

I am grateful for my low-grade fever. It calls me to catch up on much-needed sleep. *Amen* to that!

My thoughts:

_____
_____
_____
_____
_____

Additional key words: SLEEP and REST

Instant Gratitude

February 20

I am grateful my immune system is getting more and more robust even when I am around others who are sick. Thank goodness for effective self-care habits!

My thoughts:

_____
_____
_____
_____
_____

Additional key words: BODY CARE

February 21

I am grateful the Universe keeps bringing me sounds of beautiful laughter—those of others and my own—that inspire me to rise out of bed each morning. Symphony of sweetness!

My thoughts:

_____
_____
_____
_____
_____

Additional key words: PROSPERITY and ABUNDANCE / HIGHER POWER and UNIVERSE

Instant Gratitude

February 22

I am grateful for the energizing song, "What Makes You Beautiful." It's pop, but cool. I choose to create a lively environment that supports me through my day.

My thoughts:

_____
_____
_____
_____
_____

Additional key words: FUN and LAUGHTER

February 23

I am grateful for restaurants that serve fresh foods. My body loves easy-to-digest meals that it can quickly convert into energy.

My thoughts:
_____
_____
_____
_____
_____

Additional key words: FOOD and NUTRIENTS

Instant Gratitude

February 24

I am grateful for my toilet. I could pee in a cup or poop in a bucket, but just for today, I'll treasure my porcelain throne.

My thoughts:

_____
_____
_____
_____
_____

Additional key words: PROSPERITY and ABUNDANCE

February 25

I am grateful for slippery situations (temptations) that wake me up to the truth about my weaknesses. To save myself from falling, I curl up in my Creator's palm and find genuine comfort and rest.

My thoughts:

_____
_____
_____
_____
_____

Additional key words: SPIRIT and SOUL / HIGHER POWER and UNIVERSE

Instant Gratitude

February 26

I am grateful for one of my favorite lines in a TV show, *Psych*. A woman says to her boyfriend, "Stop acting like a child!" to which he replies, "I am *not acting!*" Today and every day, I honor the kid in me.

My thoughts:

_____
_____
_____
_____
_____

Additional key words: CHILD-LIKE JOY

February 27

I am grateful to have the support of many spiritually rich people who bless my journey with their presence. This is prosperity beyond my wildest dreams!

My thoughts:

_____
_____
_____
_____
_____

Additional key words: SUPPORT TEAM / PROSPERITY and ABUNDANCE

Instant Gratitude

February 28

I am grateful for my new drawer-less desk. A streamlined, clutter-free workspace is a healthy move for me, mentally, physically, and spiritually. *Less is more.*

My thoughts:

_____
_____
_____
_____
_____

Additional key words: MINDSET / SPIRIT and SOUL

February 29 (Leap Year)

I am grateful for my attitude of gratitude. By acknowledging the bright side of every dark situation, I can access energy and wisdom, which fuel me into action.

My thoughts:

_____
_____
_____
_____
_____

Additional key words: COURAGE and ACTION

Instant Gratitude

March 1

I am grateful for reminders to pace myself in everything. My goal is to cross finish lines with grace, ease, and laughter.

My thoughts:

_____

_____

_____

_____

_____

Additional key words: MINDSET / BODY CARE

# March 2

I am grateful for the patience and wisdom God has been pouring into me since I landed in a wheelchair and began this amazing journey of rebuilding my body from the inside out. Surrender does lead to victory!

My thoughts:

_____
_____
_____
_____
_____

Additional key words: HIGHER POWER and UNIVERSE

March 3

I am grateful that at any time I can take three deep breaths, close my eyes, and be on a beach absorbing limitless fresh air and sunshine.

My thoughts:

_____
_____
_____
_____
_____

Additional key words: SPIRIT and SOUL / NATURE and WEATHER

March 4

I am grateful that I've finally come to fully believe that "slow and steady wins the race." Panic, rush, and crush are old friends who served me well in getting me to where I am now.

❈

Dear Reader: What thought or belief within you might drive you to spend energy to the point of exhaustion? Let's ask for courage to face those subconscious thoughts and beliefs so we can feel fantastic in our bodies—and look great!

My thoughts:

_____
_____
_____
_____
_____

Additional key words: MINDSET

Instant Gratitude

March 5

I am grateful for friends who speak up, take action, and laugh with authenticity. Witnessing their trust in their higher power inspires awe.

My thoughts:

_____
_____
_____
_____
_____

Additional key words: SUPPORT TEAM / HIGHER POWER and UNIVERSE

March 6

I am grateful for every minute in which I am willing to focus on fantastic moments; creating and remembering joy helps me to gain relief from pain.

My thoughts:

Additional key words: FUN and LAUGHTER / BODY / PAIN

Instant Gratitude

March 7

I am grateful that just a slight modification in food can make a great difference in my feeling better in my body!

My thoughts:

_____
_____
_____
_____
_____

Additional key words: FOOD and NUTRIENTS / BODY

March 8

I am grateful I don't have a bladder infection or a kidney stone, *and* my poop is looking pretty darn good.

My thoughts:

_____
_____
_____
_____
_____

Additional key words: BODY CARE

March 9

I am grateful my brain does not need to make all my decisions. Great Spirit flows wisdom into my gut and brilliantly arranges everything, like perfect timing, resources, and space.

❈

Dear Reader: Can you recall a time when *not* listening to your gut intuition created problems and even cost you money? Let's pause to breathe deeply several times today and truly follow our gut and divine guidance.

My thoughts:

_____
_____
_____
_____
_____

Additional key words: WISDOM and INTUITION / HIGHER POWER and UNIVERSE / MONEY

March 10

I am grateful for my joy-goggles! Wearing these lenses does *not* mean I sweep anger, envy, and sadness under the rug but seek and celebrate silver linings *everywhere!*

My thoughts:

_____
_____
_____
_____
_____

Additional key words: CHILD-LIKE JOY

March 11

I am grateful for reminders that everything I perceive is just that—my point of view in the moment. When I change my perception, I change my world. Yippee!

❀

Dear Reader: Is there something you would like to change in the world around you? Let's begin by changing what is *within* ourselves so we can celebrate seeing changes *beyond* us.

My thoughts:

_____
_____
_____
_____
_____

Additional key words: MINDSET

March 12

I am grateful for fantastically fresh air after a rainfall. When I step outside and take a deep breath, it feels like God cleansed the air just for me.

My thoughts:

___

___

___

___

___

Additional key words: NATURE and WEATHER

Instant Gratitude

March 13

I am grateful for courage to speak up and change *my* behavior whenever someone is not respecting my time or effort. I can't change others, but I *can* take action to improve my own quality of life.

My thoughts:

___
___
___
___
___

Additional key words: HEALTHY BOUNDARIES / COURAGE and ACTION

March 14

I am grateful for the Ancient Hawaiian prayer of reconciliation, Ho'oponopono: "I am sorry. Please forgive me. Thank you. I love you."

My thoughts:

_____
_____
_____
_____
_____

Additional key words: SPIRIT and SOUL

Instant Gratitude

March 15

I am grateful for the ability to change my lenses and see the "forest" perspective. Problems are not problems when I leave tunnel vision behind.

My thoughts:

Additional key words: MINDSET

March 16

I am grateful that the sun rises when it rises and I no longer struggle for things to be different than they are. Mmm...*this* must be serenity.

My thoughts:

___

___

___

___

___

Additional key words: MINDSET / NATURE and WEATHER

Instant Gratitude

March 17

I am grateful for my sobriety across the board. There is no way I could enjoy rock-solid, loving people in my life if I were lost in booze, lust, sex, carbs, drugs, or spending money as if today was my last day on Earth. *Zowie!*

❈

Dear Reader: What fantastic decisions are you making for yourself today that also benefit others around you during your visit on this planet? Let's choose *deliberate recovery,* "consciously following our gut intuition and taking bite-sized steps to invite life-affirming nutrients into the body, mind, and spirit simultaneously" (from *Birth of a Self-Care Vigilante,* p. 224).

My thoughts:

_____
_____
_____
_____
_____

Additional key words: VICTORY and CELEBRATION / GUT INTUITION / SELF-CARE

March 18

I am grateful that my quest for sanity requires me to look for something new about myself to love and cherish each day. Insanity wants me dead and done; to that I say, "That's no fun!"

My thoughts:

_____
_____
_____
_____
_____

Additional key words: SPIRIT and SOUL / SELF-WORTH

Instant Gratitude

March 19

I am grateful for cheerful music and healthy bowel movements—but not necessarily in that order!

My thoughts:

_____
_____
_____
_____
_____

Additional key words: FUN and LAUGHTER

March 20

I am grateful that happiness is not about waiting for something or someone else to make me happy. It's about me cracking me up!

My thoughts:

_____
_____
_____
_____
_____

Additional key words: FUN and LAUGHTER

Instant Gratitude

March 21

I am grateful that new angels *in human form* keep showing themselves to me. Perhaps it is because I welcome comforting, creative energy into my everyday life.

My thoughts:

_____
_____
_____
_____
_____

Additional key words: SPIRIT and SOUL / SUPPORT TEAM

March 22

I am grateful my attitude of gratitude can carry me through bouts of mild depression. Thank goodness I can help dissolve lethargy in my body and indifference in my mind with frequent doses of laughter and acts of self-compassion.

My thoughts:

_____
_____
_____
_____
_____

Additional key words: SPIRIT and SOUL / FUN and LAUGHTER

Instant Gratitude

March 23

I am grateful for deeply grounded yet light-hearted people on this planet. Hearing their soothing voices leads to my feeling hope for humankind.

My thoughts:

_____
_____
_____
_____
_____

Additional key words: SUPPORT TEAM

March 24

I am grateful to be surrounded by hope-filled people who have goals. Some days they rub off on me, and on others I rub off on them. It's *all* good!

❀

Dear Reader: What hours during the day or days of the week do you feel alone and unmotivated? Let's identify our "lull times" and reignite hope by remembering the individuals who spend a lot of time doing what we would like to accomplish *and* by taking at least one bite-sized action toward our goal(s).

My thoughts:

_____
_____
_____
_____
_____

Additional key words: SUPPORT TEAM / PURPOSE

Instant Gratitude

March 25

I am grateful to remember that I can start a new day at any moment. This attitude keeps me fresh and hopeful!

My thoughts:

_____

_____

_____

_____

_____

Additional key words: MINDSET

March 26

I am grateful I can have conversations with my future self to help me make decisions today. Priorities come through with clarity.

My thoughts:

_____
_____
_____
_____
_____

Additional key words: SPIRIT and SOUL

Instant Gratitude

March 27

I am grateful that my moments of wild spontaneity do not lead to chaos anymore. Instead, my adventurous moments lead to laughter and success!

My thoughts:

_____
_____
_____
_____
_____

Additional key words: SPIRIT and SOUL / FUN and LAUGHTER

March 28

I am grateful for the influx of creative, wise, and humorous mentors into my life. Universe is just ridiculously serious about my having pleasure and purpose on Earth!

My thoughts:

Additional key words: INSPIRATION and CREATIVITY / ROLE MODELS

Instant Gratitude

March 29

I am grateful for my deep appreciation for the time I have left on this planet. Everything is one pitch at a time (sending) or one catch at a time (receiving). It's all about the *flow* in the moment—breath, blood, and body.

My thoughts:

_____
_____
_____
_____
_____

Additional key words: TIME / SPORTS and ATHLETICS

March 30

I am grateful for drivers, pilots, and conductors who are sober physically and emotionally. Public health and safety begins with vigilant self-care.

My thoughts:

_____
_____
_____
_____
_____

Additional key words: PUBLIC HEALTH and SAFETY

Instant Gratitude

March 31

I am grateful for my ability to filter out what I truly need to hear versus what is *exquisite noise pollution* (influx of attractive information that may not serve me well). De-cluttering my brain with meditation keeps me clear, serene, and sane.

My thoughts:

_____
_____
_____
_____
_____

Additional key words: MINDSET / PRAYER and MEDITATION

April 1

I am grateful I no longer obsess over sex or sugar—wait, *who am I?* A child of God who knows she's being cared for, one day at a time.

My thoughts:

_____
_____
_____
_____
_____

Additional key words: SPIRIT and SOUL / HIGHER POWER and UNIVERSE

Instant Gratitude

April 2

I am grateful for my rockin'-awesome role models who train from the inside out—starting with fitness in the kitchen and meditation before working out.

My thoughts:

_____
_____
_____
_____
_____

Additional key words: ROLE MODELS / BODY CARE

April 3

I am grateful for my belief that spiritual fitness is key to sustaining long-term mental and physical fitness.

My thoughts:

_____
_____
_____
_____
_____

Additional key words: SPIRIT and SOUL / BODY CARE

April 4

I am grateful for willingness to detox my body when underlying anger reveals itself through negative thoughts, poor food choices, and resistance to relaxation. Thank you, my inner rebel, for allowing me the chance to set things right and let go of what I truly do not need.

❈

Dear Reader: Might you have a habit or resentment that you are ready to drop and wish to stop the creation of toxins within your body? Let's focus on letting them go by breathing deeply, stretching, nourishing our bodies with food and rest, writing, talking with others, praying and meditating, and making amends to ourselves and others with compassion.

My thoughts:

_____

_____

_____

_____

_____

Additional key words: MINDSET / BODY CARE

April 5

I am grateful for fresh basil and cilantro! They are so yummy, beautiful, and healing for me in so many ways!

My thoughts:

_____
_____
_____
_____
_____

Additional key words: FOOD and NUTRIENTS

Instant Gratitude

April 6

I am grateful that drinking water, stretching, and tapping to support the health of my beautiful internal organs increases my ability to live to the fullest today!

My thoughts:

_____
_____
_____
_____
_____

Additional key words: BODY CARE

April 7

I am grateful for my renewed enthusiasm for life. A baby's laughter, as well as other delightful surprises, reminds me of the Universe's limitless generosity.

My thoughts:

_____
_____
_____
_____
_____

Additional key words: PROSPERITY and ABUNDANCE

Instant Gratitude

April 8

I am grateful that no matter how spun out I can get, reading prayers and meditation passages always takes me to a higher level of consciousness. I welcome these *big hugs* from God.

My thoughts:

_____
_____
_____
_____
_____

Additional key words: PRAYER and MEDITATION / HIGHER POWER and UNIVERSE

April 9

I am grateful for reminders to pace myself in working wisely, playing hard, and resting well. Like facing one pitch at a time, I put my heart into each and every moment.

My thoughts:

_____
_____
_____
_____
_____

Additional key words: BODY CARE

Instant Gratitude

April 10

I am grateful I can giggle and laugh myself silly—Woohoo!—*especially* during difficult times. Stress relief is vital to happiness!

My thoughts:

_____

_____

_____

_____

_____

Additional key words: FUN and LAUGHTER

April 11

I am grateful I now feel *so complete* inside and yet look forward to even happier days.

My thoughts:

_____
_____
_____
_____
_____

Additional key words: SPIRIT and SOUL.

April 12

I am grateful I can quickly stop fear-driven stories in my head from ruining my day. Switching radio stations from KFER to KLAF stimulates higher vibrational frequencies throughout my body and produces thoughts like, "I'm so glad to be alive!"

❈

Dear Reader: What used to be scary or intimidating to you but you overcame those feelings? Let's remember the victories and use the higher vibrations of joy to produce even more goodies!

My thoughts:

_____
_____
_____
_____
_____

Additional key words: MINDSET

April 13

I am grateful for reminders that even the tiniest improvement in my daily self-care regimen can reap great rewards when I least expect them. Yay for natural bursts of energy!

My thoughts:

_____
_____
_____
_____
_____

Additional key words: BODY CARE

Instant Gratitude

April 14

I am grateful I have more options than I think, even when I am between a rock and a hard place. Dial into the Universe for amazing results!

My thoughts:

_____
_____
_____
_____
_____

Additional key words: MINDSET / HIGHER POWER and UNIVERSE

April 15

I am grateful to have heard through a morning meditation: "Letting go is the best way to receive." Today, I'll consciously clear my mind to invite serenity and prosperity.

My thoughts:

_____
_____
_____
_____
_____

Additional key words: PRAYER and MEDITATION

April 16

I am grateful for willingness to take bite-sized actions that may not appear to get me far, but then *voilà!* I have suddenly crossed the finish line!

❁

Dear Reader: What actions could you take to pursue life experiences you desire? Let's write down our "bucket list" of dreams and pray for guidance on taking steps to make it a reality!

My thoughts:

_____
_____
_____
_____
_____

Additional key words: VICTORY and CELEBRATION

April 17

I am grateful for evidence of my inner joy—waking up to the sound of my own laughter. In my dream, Kermit's face was making contortions; in my Miss Piggy voice, I lovingly responded, "Kermeee!" OK. So maybe I could use a meeting.

My thoughts:

_____
_____
_____
_____
_____

Additional key words: FUN and LAUGHTER

Instant Gratitude

April 18

I am grateful I no longer feel the need to be right about everything all the time. Thank goodness for the freedom to be wrong and perfectly imperfect!

My thoughts:

_____
_____
_____
_____
_____

Additional key words: MINDSET

April 19

I am grateful for willingness to set aside my tiara and let an infinite source of creativity *surprise* me with new unimaginable experiences!

My thoughts:

_____
_____
_____
_____
_____

Additional key words: INSPIRATION and CREATIVITY

Instant Gratitude

April 20

I am grateful for the true deliciousness of sleep. I used to feel that sleep meant missing out on something exciting. Now, it is clear that my Creator is planting great ideas into my subconscious mind and restoring light into my body.

My thoughts:

_____
_____
_____
_____
_____

Additional key words: SLEEP and REST / HIGHER POWER and UNIVERSE

April 21

I am grateful that with each slow and gentle deep breath I can fill my soul with waves of nature's bounty: blue skies with puffy clouds, untouched sand dunes, aromatic forests, and relaxing waters. This is richness that stays with me forever.

My thoughts:

___

___

___

___

___

Additional key words: NATURE and WEATHER / SLEEP and REST / CHILD-LIKE JOY / MONEY / FUN

Instant Gratitude

April 22

I am grateful for answers and solutions that appear when I least expect them. Prayer, meditation, and footwork truly invite miracles!

My thoughts:

_____
_____
_____
_____
_____

Additional key words: PRAYER and MEDITATION

April 23

I am grateful that when I focus on breathing deeply in all my actions, these moment-by-moment victories dissolve my fear of success. Woohoo, God *rocks!*

My thoughts:

___

___

___

___

___

Additional key words: VICTORY and CELEBRATION

Instant Gratitude

April 24

I am grateful for my free car wash today. Rain does hide sunshine, but I will allow sunshine in my heart to carry me throughout the day!

My thoughts:

_____
_____
_____
_____
_____

Additional key words: NATURE and WEATHER

April 25

I am grateful I truly believe that we live in an abundant Universe, and so I can kiss self-deprivation "Good-bye!"

❈

Dear Reader: Do you have a daily practice of deep breathing in which you inhale all the stars, planets, sun, and moon into your body and exhale your worries? Let's expand our breath to expand our world and witness what a difference this makes!

My thoughts:

_____
_____
_____
_____
_____

Additional key words: PROSPERITY and ABUNDANCE

Instant Gratitude

April 26

I am grateful to able to feel good about myself even when people are picky, cranky, and irrational. I've got "water off a duck's back" serenity. Ahh!

My thoughts:

_____
_____
_____
_____
_____

Additional key words: SPIRIT and SOUL / MINDSET

April 27

I am grateful to have rigorously honest people in my world. My life is too short for fluffy excuses and elaborate stories. Truth *rocks*!

My thoughts:

Additional key words: SUPPORT TEAM

Instant Gratitude

April 28

I am grateful for wisdom from mentors I admire and follow. They light a fire under my butt and ignite me into action!

My thoughts:

_____
_____
_____
_____
_____

Additional key words: SUPPORT TEAM / COURAGE and ACTION

April 29

I am grateful that every challenge I have faced has expanded my skill set and *increased* my "marketability." Who would've thunk?

My thoughts:

_____
_____
_____
_____
_____

Additional key words: VICTORY and CELEBRATION

Instant Gratitude

April 30

I am grateful for gloomy days; they make other days even brighter. Today, I choose to celebrate *no matter what!*

My thoughts:

_____
_____
_____
_____
_____

Additional key words: PROSPERITY and ABUNDANCE

May 1

I am grateful that my desire for real freedom overpowers my physical cravings. During tough times I focus on being a role model I admire. My guardian angels then bless me with relief and renewed inspiration.

❀

Dear Reader: During tough times, what kinds of slogans do you use to help you get through pain, anger, or worry? Let's share fun slogans with others so that we all can overcome challenges with grace, ease, and laughter!

My thoughts:

_____
_____
_____
_____
_____

Additional key words: SPIRIT and SOUL / ROLE MODELS

Instant Gratitude

May 2

I am grateful that I am *me*. I don't want to have someone else's face, body, job, home, higher power, etc. Emerging as the real me (and leaving the kaka behind) is surprisingly enjoyable!

My thoughts:

_____
_____
_____
_____
_____

Additional key words: SELF-WORTH

May 3

I am grateful for both the adult and the kid in me. Let me try that again: I love the kid in me and am thankful for when my grown-up side shows up to help her *shine*!

My thoughts:

_____
_____
_____
_____
_____

Additional key words: CHILD-LIKE JOY

May 4

I am grateful that every time my world turns upside down, I remember that something surprisingly wonderful will come from it. *Seek and you shall find.* How divine!

My thoughts:

_____
_____
_____
_____
_____

Additional key words: MINDSET

May 5

I am grateful for my active determination to let go of any stress in my body. In fact, I think I'll go to the bathroom now and then make some tea. Yep, I'm *that* easy.

My thoughts:

_____
_____
_____
_____
_____

Additional key words: BODY

May 6

I am grateful to hear the delightful ringing of laughter in the voices of people I spend time with on the phone or in person. There is an angel within every one of us. Let us share divine comfort and joy!

My thoughts:

_____
_____
_____
_____
_____

Additional key words: SUPPORT TEAM and SPIRIT / SOUL

May 7

I am grateful for dark green veggies. They help to keep my sinuses and intestines happy—which puts me in a good mood!

Dear Reader: If given a choice between eating something fresh or something preserved (in a package), which would you choose? Let's select fresh food to nourish brain and body as often as possible.

My thoughts:

_____
_____
_____
_____
_____

Additional key words: FOOD and NUTRIENTS

Instant Gratitude

May 8

I am grateful for expressions of God's grace, forgiveness, and love through fresh air and sunshine, healing time with a friend, and a surprise kiss from a puppy. Heaven.

My thoughts:

_____
_____
_____
_____
_____

Additional key words: HIGHER POWER and UNIVERSE / NATURE and WEATHER / SUPPORT TEAM

May 9

I am grateful for gorgeous sunsets, especially as the clouds part after the rain and the golden-pink glow bursts through!

My thoughts:

_____
_____
_____
_____
_____

Additional key words: NATURE and WEATHER

Instant Gratitude

May 10

I am grateful to realize that the Creator of the majestic Red Rocks of Sedona also made me. I see human shapes in these rocks, and this magnificence is also in *us*.

My thoughts:

_____
_____
_____
_____
_____

Additional key words: NATURE / HIGHER POWER

May 11

I am grateful for the little things in life, like a good poop. *It's not overrated!* Letting it go helps me feel marvelous and light.

❖

Dear Reader: What changes can you make regarding food, exercise, or self-expression to invite greater vitality, visibility, and victory in your life? Let's consciously care for our intestines to boost our immune systems.

My thoughts:

_____
_____
_____
_____
_____

Additional key words: MINDSET / BODY CARE

Instant Gratitude

May 12

I am grateful that my friends integrate fun into their daily lives as I do. This makes the world a whole lot sweeter!

My thoughts:

_____
_____
_____
_____
_____

Additional key words: SUPPORT TEAM / FUN and LAUGHTER

May 13

I am grateful for all the wonderful clues and nudges the Universe offers me in handling complicated situations. I'm glad I can give my ego a rest and follow divine guidance!

My thoughts:

_____
_____
_____
_____
_____

Additional key words: HIGHER POWER and UNIVERSE

Instant Gratitude

May 14

I am grateful my family is beginning to see the light: a connection between fresh food and better health. Sometimes they are even willing to eat their veggies. Amen. *Hallelujah!*

My thoughts:

_____

_____

_____

_____

_____

Additional key words: FAMILY / FOOD and NUTRIENTS

May 15

I am grateful for my enthusiasm to learn new techniques for moving energy and gaining strength within my body. It really is an inside job!

My thoughts:

_____
_____
_____
_____
_____

Additional key words: BODY CARE

Instant Gratitude

May 16

I am grateful for this incredible feeling of being connected to the Universe, especially with every living creature and object that shares vibrant energy. Today, let's hold hands in spirit and move forward together!

My thoughts:

___

___

___

___

___

Additional key words: HIGHER POWER and UNIVERSE / SPIRIT and SOUL

May 17

I am grateful that as much as I enjoy adult privileges, like driving a car and making money, I still love lying on the grass, staring at the sky, and taking naps whenever I please.

❖

Dear Reader: What can you do today to stay in physical contact with Mother Earth and absorb nourishing energy? Let's bring more natural elements into our homes: plants for cleaner air, hot water or sand for our feet, and stones for healing meditations or massages.

My thoughts:

_____
_____
_____
_____
_____

Additional key words: NATURE and WEATHER / SLEEP and REST / CHILD-LIKE JOY

Instant Gratitude

May 18

I am grateful for a long-overdue lunch at an outdoor café *by myself*. With warm sunshine on my face and the soothing sounds of a bubbling fountain, I am restored. What a slice of heaven on earth!

My thoughts:

_____
_____
_____
_____
_____

Additional key words: SPIRIT and SOUL

May 19

I am grateful for non-GMO foods and restaurants. Happy intestines, happy life!

My thoughts:

_____
_____
_____
_____
_____

Additional key words: FOOD and NUTRIENTS

Instant Gratitude

May 20

I am grateful I am not God nor am I responsible for God's "to do" list, which most likely is short: "create people and shine some sun, water, and love upon them so they may bask in my Light." Yup, "Let go and let God."

❀

Dear Reader: Can you think of any positive results that might happen if you stop adding someone else's job to your "to do" list and let go of any self-blame for the past or present? Let's stretch out our arms, chest, and legs now to release stress and to send wonderful blood to our hearts and lungs.

My thoughts:

_____
_____
_____
_____
_____

Additional key words: HIGHER POWER and UNIVERSE / BODY CARE

May 21

I am grateful my life is not about becoming perfect. Getting better and better is perfect enough!

My thoughts:

_____

_____

_____

_____

_____

Additional key words: SPIRIT and SOUL

Instant Gratitude

May 22

I am grateful that by consciously and subconsciously letting go of old ideas, beliefs, and belongings, I make space for great thoughts, experiences, and opportunities!

My thoughts:

_____
_____
_____
_____
_____

Additional key words: SPIRIT and SOUL

May 23

I am grateful to be overcoming my fear of success. While acknowledging my accomplishments each day, I can see that the sky is *not* falling after all. Whew!

❊

Dear Reader: Is there something you need to do that bookending (see January 7) would assist you in accomplishing sooner than later? Let's get things done *today* with grace, ease, and laughter.

My thoughts:

_____
_____
_____
_____
_____

Additional key words: VICTORY and CELEBRATION / SELF-WORTH

Instant Gratitude

May 24

I am grateful I did everything I did not feel like doing yesterday, because showing up where I was needed brought me many nice surprises. Letting go of self-centered fear leads to heart-centered delight!

My thoughts:

_____
_____
_____
_____
_____

Additional key words: PROSPERITY and ABUNDANCE

May 25

I am grateful for the healing of my esophagus and voice box, thanks to my vigilant self-care. Being able to speak, ask for what I need, and share my visions saves my soul.

My thoughts:

_____
_____
_____
_____
_____

Additional key words: BODY CARE / SPIRIT and SOUL

May 26

I am grateful for truly grounded, feet-firmly-planted people. By staying close to them, I feel inspired to connect deeper to the earth's core while receiving light from above. *We are trees!*

My thoughts:

_____
_____
_____
_____
_____

Additional key words: SUPPORT TEAM / NATURE and WEATHER

May 27

I am grateful my eyes are open to *oodles* of blessings that come my way every moment of every day. Living in the present, no matter how tough things get, is so rewarding!

My thoughts:

_____
_____
_____
_____
_____

Additional key words: PROSPERITY and ABUNDANCE

Instant Gratitude

May 28

I am grateful to remember that good car care is good self-care. I am safe and comfortable in a well-maintained vehicle: healthy engine (heart), tires (great shoes), clean windows (vision), and gas (energy for the day)!

My thoughts:

_____
_____
_____
_____
_____

Additional key words: PROSPERITY and ABUNDANCE

May 29

I am grateful for my ability to stop eating when my stomach has had enough. No longer stuffing it past "full" keeps me feeling light and energetic. Yay—I finally have a *stop button!*

My thoughts:

_____
_____
_____
_____
_____

Additional key words: BODY

Instant Gratitude

May 30

I am grateful for soldiers, dead or alive, abroad or at home. Special thanks to prisoners of war and to those who are missing in action. Blessings to you and your loved ones!

My thoughts:

_____
_____
_____
_____
_____

Additional key words: ROLE MODELS

June 1

I am grateful for gold nuggets of wisdom revealed to me as I track my time and activities throughout the day. Prosperous time consciousness leads to higher levels of performance!

❖

Dear Reader: What is one fantasy in your mind that pulls you away from taking good care of yourself and loved ones? Let's track our time regularly throughout the day to stay focused on priorities that benefit many people.

My thoughts:

_____
_____
_____
_____
_____

Additional key words: TIME / WISDOM and INTUITION

Instant Gratitude

June 2

I am grateful for the guts to take charge of my time. By staying in tune with the Universe, I detach from distractions and protect my priorities!

My thoughts:

_____
_____
_____
_____
_____

Additional key words: TIME / HIGHER POWER and UNIVERSE

June 3

I am grateful for people on my support team who redirect attention back to my well-being and personal strengths, even amidst crises and challenges with my health, home, and outside world.

❖

Dear Reader: What could you do for yourself to gain greater confidence in your health while being around people who may be ill and contagious? Let's stay consciously connected with what our bodies need to be as robust as possible.

My thoughts:

_____
_____
_____
_____
_____

Additional key words: SUPPORT TEAM

Instant Gratitude

June 4

I am grateful that when I am grumpy and don't feel like being grateful, the habit kicks in and puts me in a better headspace *in spite of myself*!

My thoughts:

_____
_____
_____
_____
_____

Additional key words: MINDSET

June 5

I am grateful that people view me as a good luck charm. I love hearing about their new jobs, promotions, projects, contracts, classes, shows, and relationships. Together, we celebrate prosperity that comes from practicing vigilant self-care!

My thoughts:

_____
_____
_____
_____
_____

Additional key words: VICTORY and CELEBRATION

Instant Gratitude

June 6

I am grateful for mustard. It adds the perfect zing to any bite of my food. Yup, I am *that* easy!

My thoughts:

_____
_____
_____
_____
_____

Additional key words: FOOD and NUTRIENTS

June 7

I am grateful for my left brain. The right one gets all the glory for creative accomplishments, but it's *the left one* that delivers me across the finish line!

My thoughts:

_____
_____
_____
_____
_____

Additional key words: MINDSET / VICTORY and CELEBRATION

Instant Gratitude

June 8

I am grateful that when my mind gets constipated, stretching my body from head to toe helps me to unbundle stuck energy and awaken my genius again!

My thoughts:

_____
_____
_____
_____
_____

Additional key words: MINDSET / BODY CARE

June 9

I am grateful for my awesomely clear mind—free of brain fog and limited impulse control. Good-bye, bread; hello, sunshine!

My thoughts:

_____
_____
_____
_____
_____

Additional key words: MINDSET / NUTRITION

Instant Gratitude

June 10

I am grateful for the willingness to speak from my heart at all times, welcoming opportunities for my "gratitude lantern" to shine upon the Universe's limitless power and blessings.

My thoughts:

_____
_____
_____
_____
_____

Additional key words: HIGHER POWER and UNIVERSE

June 11

I am grateful to realize that the only person who is blocking me from freely being myself is me. One contrary action at a time, I transform my excuse-making machine into a "Let's jive!" machine.

❀

Dear Reader: Can you think of any positive results that might happen if you stop blaming yourself for something in the past? Let's stretch out our arms, chest, and legs now and send wonderful blood to our heart and lungs.

My thoughts:

_____
_____
_____
_____
_____

Additional key words: COURAGE and ACTION

Instant Gratitude

June 12

I am grateful that laughter, among other things, fills my emotional fuel tank every day. With it, I can perpetuate a loving and caring environment wherever I go.

My thoughts:

_____
_____
_____
_____
_____

Additional key words: FUN and LAUGHTER

June 13

I am grateful to be able to laugh so hard that it hurts *so good*. Bring it on, world, bring it on!

My thoughts:

_____
_____
_____
_____
_____

Additional key words: FUN and LAUGHTER

Instant Gratitude

June 14

I am grateful for the willingness to donate blood. I can't stop natural or human tragedies, but I *can* offer a second chance at life, as I was given one when I was a newborn baby.

My thoughts:

_____
_____
_____
_____
_____

Additional key words: PROSPERITY and ABUNDANCE

June 15

I am grateful for my healthy vocal cords. When they were inflamed and "locked," it hurt to laugh even slightly. I can now laugh to "pee-point" *whenever* I want!

❦

Dear Reader: What time of the day or night do you need more nourishment (sleep, food, people, nature) to feel vibrant and productive? Let's frequently ask our bodies, "Body, what do you need right now?" We listen and respond with kindness.

My thoughts:

_____
_____
_____
_____
_____

Additional key words: FUN and LAUGHTER / BODY CARE

Instant Gratitude

June 16

I am grateful for finding new ways for my internal organs to get happy and to stay happy. People I love deserve to be with a healthy, compassionate me!

My thoughts:

_____
_____
_____
_____
_____

Additional key words: BODY CARE / PUBLIC HEALTH AND SAFETY / FAMILY

June 17

I am grateful for the abundance of opportunities to laugh. It gets a bit crazy sometimes, but it's worth it.

My thoughts:

_____
_____
_____
_____
_____

Additional key words: FUN and LAUGHTER

Instant Gratitude

June 18

I am grateful for my imagination. It used to get me into trouble. Now, it brings me to new places where I belong and thrive.

My thoughts:

_____
_____
_____
_____
_____

Additional key words: PROSPERITY and ABUNDANCE

June 19

I am grateful for *not* always getting what I want *when* I want it. Obviously, the Universe has something better in store for me. I will keep cultivating healthy energy within so that I can be ready to rise to the occasion.

My thoughts:

_____
_____
_____
_____
_____

Additional key words: HIGHER POWER and UNIVERSE

June 20

I am grateful for the feeling that I can do cartwheels—at least in my mind. Happiness is *so* refreshing!

❋

Dear Reader: Do you believe that we can feel young at heart at any age? Let's dissolve any preconceived notions about what our lives should look like at each age and take special care of our internal organs. *Happy organs, happy life!*

My thoughts:

_____
_____
_____
_____
_____

Additional key words: MINDSET

June 21

I am grateful for my willingness to let go of trying to be perfect when it is not a life-or-death situation. Perfectionism can lead to lower productivity and loss of time, and we just can't have that!

My thoughts:

_____
_____
_____
_____
_____

Additional key words: SPIRIT and SOUL

Instant Gratitude

June 22

I am grateful to be who I am today. All my ducks might not be in a row, but hey—life is short. I have got to live it with compassion and laughter . . . 'til I drop!

My thoughts:

_____

_____

_____

_____

_____

Additional key words: SELF-WORTH / FUN and LAUGHTER

June 23

I am grateful for people who encourage me to rest and relax, especially when I struggle to make time for self-care and self-investment.

My thoughts:

Additional key words: SUPPORT TEAM / SLEEP and REST

Instant Gratitude

June 24

I am grateful that I frequently validate myself *from within* and no longer rely on approval from others to feel fantastic. I am *one* with the Universe!

My thoughts:

_____
_____
_____
_____
_____

Additional key words: SELF-WORTH / HIGHER POWER and UNIVERSE

June 25

I am grateful for friends who have faith in marriage and nurture laughter in their journey with their special someone.

My thoughts:

_____
_____
_____
_____
_____

Additional key words: FUN and LAUGHTER / FAMILY / SUPPORT TEAM

Instant Gratitude

June 26

I am grateful for reminders that, as someone who compulsively fantasizes, I need to stay spiritually fit to protect my physical and emotional sobriety. Honesty *rocks*!

My thoughts:

_____
_____
_____
_____
_____

Additional key words: SPIRIT and SOUL

June 27

I am grateful for the ability and freedom to pray anywhere and anytime. God *loves* hearing from me (as if He has a choice)!

My thoughts:

_____
_____
_____
_____
_____

Additional key words: PRAYER and MEDITATION / HIGHER POWER and UNIVERSE

Instant Gratitude

June 28

I am grateful for sober friends who love me so much that they call me first thing in the morning to sing show tunes at the top of their lungs like there's no tomorrow. I am *loving* my second childhood!

My thoughts:

_____
_____
_____
_____
_____

Additional key words: SUPPORT TEAM / FUN and LAUGHTER

June 29

I am grateful for mango. I should go pick mangoes for a living. Paradise on earth. *How juicy!*

My thoughts:

_____
_____
_____
_____
_____

Additional key words: FOOD and NUTRIENTS

June 30

I am grateful to be fit, fabulous, and fifty+, despite illness, injury, and isolation. Depression sucks, but God and I *rock!*

❁

Dear Reader: Are you ready to believe that getting older means growing wiser and having a lot of fun? Let's put on our joy-goggles and explore sweet feelings, journeys, and connections with others on Earth.

My thoughts:

_____
_____
_____
_____
_____

Additional key words: SPIRIT and SOUL

July 1

I am grateful that the more time I spend on activities that feed my spirit, my body and mind become even more willing to participate in living fully in all areas of my life.

My thoughts:

_____
_____
_____
_____
_____

Additional key words: SPIRIT and SOUL

Instant Gratitude

July 2

I am grateful for quiet, peaceful mornings. I should bottle this up and sell it!

My thoughts:

_____

_____

_____

_____

_____

Additional key words: SPIRIT and SOUL

July 3

I am grateful to realize that my most precious gift is wanting to be no one else but me, appreciating wherever I am, and adoring the people I love. God is in the house!

My thoughts:

_____
_____
_____
_____
_____

Additional key words: SELF-WORTH / HIGHER POWER and UNIVERSE

Instant Gratitude

July 4

I am grateful to see clearly that freedom needs to be fought for—liberation from old thoughts, habits, and beliefs. One day at a time, I take action to maintain and celebrate freedom inside and out.

❊

Dear Reader: Is there something you would like to do but need to get unstuck first? Let's embrace "contrary action" and do the opposite of what is typical. We *can* train our autonomic nervous system to support us in adopting healthier habits—*yes!*

My thoughts:

_____
_____
_____
_____
_____

Additional key words: MINDSET / SPIRIT and SOUL

July 5

I am grateful to crave nothing; instead, I have passion for anything placed before me. Current conditions may look bleak, but sincerity and compassion allow me to serve from a place of plenty.

My thoughts:

_____
_____
_____
_____
_____

Additional key words: PROSPERITY and ABUNDANCE / SERVICE

July 6

I am grateful to realize that downplaying my achievements to avoid arousing jealousy is not healthy or loving. God's blessings must be celebrated!

❈

Dear Reader: Are you willing to celebrate at least one thing you will achieve today? Let's share our accomplishments with someone we feel safe with and raise our vibrations of joy!

My thoughts:

___

___

___

___

___

Additional key words: SELF-WORTH / HIGHER POWER and UNIVERSE

July 7

I am grateful to remember that even though I make healthy choices with positive results, other people may not want that for themselves. Focusing my attention on those who *do* helps me *keep on smiling*.

My thoughts:

_____
_____
_____
_____
_____

Additional key words: HEALTHY BOUNDARIES

Instant Gratitude

July 8

I am grateful that when chaos is breaking loose, I can grow my energy roots more deeply into the soil, be one with Mother Nature, and feel serene.

My thoughts:

_____
_____
_____
_____
_____

Additional key words: NATURE and WEATHER

July 9

I am grateful that I can pause at any moment when I feel pulled from every direction. *Breathe!* Now I can take one right action before the next.

My thoughts:

_____
_____
_____
_____
_____

Additional key words: MINDSET / SPIRIT and SOUL

Instant Gratitude

July 10

I am grateful my body loves arugula. Every time I bite into my wonderful arugula salad, I hear from somewhere within me, "Ahh! Where have you been all my life?!?"

My thoughts:

_____

_____

_____

_____

_____

Additional key words: FOOD and NUTRIENTS

July 11

I am grateful I can go to the bathroom with ease. Stretching, drinking water, and eating well do wonders for *all* my systems!

My thoughts:

_____
_____
_____
_____
_____

Additional key words: BODY CARE / FOOD and NUTRIENTS

Instant Gratitude

July 12

I am grateful for the courage to say "No"—two little letters that spell "self-care and compassion."

❀

Dear Reader: Do you feel you need to fix, save, or rescue someone today? If so, let's make sure we are well-nourished first—mind, body, and spirit!

My thoughts:

_____
_____
_____
_____
_____

Additional key words: HEALTHY BOUNDARIES

July 13

I am grateful for an opportunity to have a yard sale and release energy that no longer belongs in my home. Making room for flowing prosperity, I feel light!

My thoughts:

_____
_____
_____
_____
_____

Additional key words: PROSPERITY and ABUNDANCE

July 14

I am grateful to eliminate *exquisite noise pollution* from my mind. Something can sound alluring and potentially true, but my gut intuition (despite my brain) will allow wisdom to emerge.

My thoughts:

___

___

___

___

___

Additional key words: MINDSET / WISDOM and INTUITION

July 15

I am grateful for easy ways to support my health (brain and body) during heat waves. Thank you, Universe, for electrolyte water, cucumbers, umbrellas, white clothing, and memories of shoveling snow in Syracuse!

My thoughts:

_____
_____
_____
_____
_____

Additional key words: BODY CARE / NATURE and WEATHER

Instant Gratitude

July 16

I am grateful for a recent reminder that taking steps backward can propel me forward. While hiking up a mountain in search of spectacular views, I needed to step downward to create new paths that led to new heights.

My thoughts:

_____
_____
_____
_____
_____

Additional key words: COURAGE and ACTION

July 17

I am grateful to find myself giggling and laughing out loud throughout the day for no apparent reason. This attitude of gratitude stuff must *really* be working!

My thoughts:

___
___
___
___
___

Additional key words: CHILD-LIKE JOY

July 18

I am grateful that I cannot make my loved ones eat gluten-free foods or go for a walk each day to overcome their illnesses. Everyone has a higher power. I let go and let God.

My thoughts:

_____
_____
_____
_____
_____

Additional key words: FOOD and NUTRIENTS/ FAMILY / HIGHER POWER and UNIVERSE

July 19

I am grateful I can embrace my rambunctiousness, boldness, and incessant curiosity—qualities that used to get me into trouble but now carry me to new levels of growth and joy. Thank you, God!

My thoughts:

_____

_____

_____

_____

_____

Additional key words: SPIRIT and SOUL / PROSPERITY and ABUNDANCE

Instant Gratitude

July 20

I am grateful I can laugh my butt off all day long and make *no apologies* for it!

My thoughts:

_____
_____
_____
_____
_____

Additional key words: FUN and LAUGHTER

July 21

I am grateful for reminders to schedule *fun time* into my everyday life, even if it's only 20 minutes of doing nothing except staring at the clouds and taking deep breaths!

My thoughts:

_____
_____
_____
_____
_____

Additional key words: TIME / SPIRIT and SOUL

Instant Gratitude

July 22

I am grateful for pain that inspires me to move, for movement is key to everything. Even when I am sitting still in meditation, Spirit stirs energy within me.

My thoughts:

_____
_____
_____
_____
_____

Additional key words: SPIRIT and SOUL / PRAYER and MEDITATION / PAIN

July 23

I am grateful for my willingness to stretch *far* beyond my comfort zone. The process may be painful, but the pleasure from great results is worth it.

❖

Dear Reader: Do you ever wonder what inventors of airplanes were thinking when they climbed into their aircrafts to lift them off the ground, or how inventors of submarines felt while stepping into a craft going under water? Let's borrow courage from our role models to jumpstart ourselves into growing it within us.

My thoughts:

_____
_____
_____
_____
_____

Additional key words: SPIRIT and SOUL / VICTORY and CELEBRATION

Instant Gratitude

July 24

I am grateful for awesome neighbors with beautiful hearts and adventurous spirits. When I didn't know where I was going, the Universe put me right where I was meant to be.

My thoughts:

_____
_____
_____
_____
_____

Additional key words: SUPPORT TEAM / HIGHER POWER and UNIVERSE

July 25

I am grateful for deep, restorative sleep, a necessity that feels luxurious to people caring for young children or sick loved ones.

My thoughts:

_____
_____
_____
_____
_____

Additional key words: SLEEP and REST

Instant Gratitude

July 26

I am grateful for surgeons who take into account patients' personal habits and arrange for follow-up care with specialists. Looking at the whole person is the way to go!

My thoughts:

___
___
___
___
___

Additional key words: PUBLIC HEALTH and SAFETY

July 27

I am grateful I have no intentions of being Wonder Woman, especially during crazy-hot hours of the day. I would rather be thinking and *being* than running around and *doing*.

My thoughts:

_____
_____
_____
_____
_____

Additional key words: NATURE and WEATHER

Instant Gratitude

July 28

I am deeply grateful for many years of quality living without alcohol. I'm sorry, my liver, for making you work hard for decades. Please forgive me for pushing beyond your limits and abandoning you. Thank you for being here for me anyway. I love you, my liver, my life!

My thoughts:

_____
_____
_____
_____
_____

Additional key words: BODY / ADDICTION

July 29

I am grateful for the courage to express things I could not say before. Good-bye, emotional constipation. *Hello, freedom!*

My thoughts:

_____
_____
_____
_____
_____

Additional key words: SPIRIT and SOUL

Instant Gratitude

July 30

I am grateful for my readiness to look at any situation from different angles. With a broadened view, new options arrive. *Yay!*

❁

Dear Reader: Have you stretched your imagination today to find solutions that could be yours? Let's set aside our assumptions and judgments to receive many good things that are truly possible.

My thoughts:

_____
_____
_____
_____
_____

Additional key words: MINDSET

July 31

I am grateful I no longer dread mornings but look forward to them with a surge of energy and enthusiasm. This is proof there *must* be a God!

My thoughts:

Additional key words: TIME / HIGHER POWER and UNIVERSE

Instant Gratitude

August 1

I am grateful for scheduled down time. When I remember to take breaks *and relax*, everyone gets a happier me!

❃

Dear Reader: What pulls you away from taking good care of yourself and loved ones? Let's track our time throughout the day and set aside time to play.

My thoughts:

_____
_____
_____
_____
_____

Additional key words: TIME / BODY CARE

August 2

I am grateful for self-appreciation with or without admiration from others. External validation weighs little because I am happy to be me!

My thoughts:

_____
_____
_____
_____
_____

Additional key words: MINDSET

Instant Gratitude

August 3

I am grateful for the chance to be on a raft going down a Class 3 rapid. Picture my crew and me: we are singing at the top of our lungs the theme song to the movie Titanic. *Priceless.*

My thoughts:

_____
_____
_____
_____
_____

Additional key words: NATURE and WEATHER / FUN and LAUGHTER

August 4

I am grateful for my willingness to ask for courage to face tasks I am insecure or not crazy about. When I open the door, the Universe delivers.

My thoughts:

_____
_____
_____
_____
_____

Additional key words: HIGHER POWER and UNIVERSE / COURAGE and ACTION

Instant Gratitude

August 5

I am grateful for the powerful light of the moon—
so mystical, magical, and mesmerizing!

My thoughts:

_____

_____

_____

_____

_____

Additional key words: CHILD-LIKE JOY

August 6

I am grateful for the feeling that I am right where I am supposed to be. Whenever my gut says that I am a little off, I can make an adjustment and get back on course.

My thoughts:

_____
_____
_____
_____
_____

Additional key words: WISDOM and INTUITION

Instant Gratitude

August 7

I am grateful for portable air cleaners. On hot, smoky, smoggy days, I take extra good care of myself by eating fresher, easier-to-digest foods and breathing cleaner air.

My thoughts:

_____
_____
_____
_____
_____

Additional key words: NATURE and WEATHER / BODY CARE

August 8

I am grateful my super-tough day is over! I learned from it and had a few laughs. "This, too, shall pass . . . like gas."

My thoughts:

_____
_____
_____
_____
_____

Additional key words: VICTORY and CELEBRATION

Instant Gratitude

August 9

I am grateful I can fall asleep instantaneously and wake up naturally after a deep sleep. Practicing self-care is a lot of work but really worthwhile!

❋

Dear Reader: What healthy habit for getting deep sleep would you like to start today? Let's reduce our exposure to blue light from computers, TV, and smartphones by resting our eyes one hour before sleep time.

My thoughts:

_____
_____
_____
_____
_____

Additional key words: SLEEP and REST

August 10

I am grateful to feel just as balanced and fully alive now that I'm back home, as I did while lying on hot, sunbaked Red Rock in Sedona. Ahh—the energy *thrives!*

My thoughts:

_____
_____
_____
_____
_____

Additional key words: PROSPERITY and ABUNDANCE

Instant Gratitude

August 11

I am grateful that spiritual fitness is a key that consistently unlocks doors all the time. I choose to use this key anytime and anywhere!

My thoughts:

_____
_____
_____
_____
_____

Additional key words: SPIRIT and SOUL

August 12

I am grateful for my non-drug-induced astounding mental clarity and serenity with no help from medication, caffeine, or nicotine. *It feels so good it should be illegal!*

My thoughts:

Additional key words: VICTORY and CELEBRATION / MINDSET

Instant Gratitude

August 13

I am grateful I search daily for things to make me laugh to "pee-point." Laughing hard enough to pee and cry is divine!

My thoughts:

_____
_____
_____
_____
_____

Additional key words: CHILD-LIKE JOY / PEE /LAUGHTER

August 14

I am grateful I listen to what my body needs for better health, even if it means disengaging from what others expect me to do. Gut intuition *rocks*!

My thoughts:

_____
_____
_____
_____
_____

Additional key words: BODY CARE / WISDOM and INTUITION

Instant Gratitude

August 15

I am grateful to have met and spent one-on-one time with really wonderful people. Thank you, Universe, for continuing to bring me folks who inspire me deeply.

My thoughts:

_____
_____
_____
_____
_____

Additional key words: SUPPORT TEAM / ROLE MODELS

August 16

I am grateful for doorframes—great stretching equipment for arms, shoulders, chest, back, legs, and more. Woohoo! It's a win-win-win-win-win situation!

❀

Dear Reader: Is there a wall, door frame, or chair you can use to keep you safe while moving your body around for greater blood flow right now? Let's use what we have in a new way to get to where we want to be.

My thoughts:

_____
_____
_____
_____
_____

Additional key words: BODY CARE

Instant Gratitude

August 17

I am grateful for reading glasses. Holy moly, it's great to see my food!

My thoughts:

_____

_____

_____

_____

_____

Additional key words: FOOD and NUTRIENTS / VICTORY and CELEBRATION

August 18

I am grateful for my little catnaps. What an amazing energy boost I get from giving myself time to pray, meditate, and recharge!

My thoughts:

_____
_____
_____
_____
_____

Additional key words: SLEEP and REST / PRAYER and MEDITATION

Instant Gratitude

August 19

I am grateful to have a new appreciation for sunrises, especially the dancing, fire-orange glow of light. This used to be my signal for bedtime, but now the sun invites me out to *shine!*

My thoughts:

_____
_____
_____
_____
_____

Additional key words: NATURE

August 20

I am grateful I no longer expect myself to remember or know everything. A connection with the Great Spirit of the Universe feeds me whatever info, strength, or wisdom I need *when* I need it. Being anxiety-free feels *awesome*!

My thoughts:

_____
_____
_____
_____
_____

Additional key words: SPIRIT and SOUL / HIGHER POWER and UNIVERSE

Instant Gratitude

August 21

I am grateful for my patience with electronic gadgets. They work funny and so do *I*.

My thoughts:

_____
_____
_____
_____
_____

Additional key words: MINDSET

August 22

I am grateful for highly imaginative, passionate, and reliable people who support me in bringing creative projects to life!

My thoughts:

_____

_____

_____

_____

_____

Additional key words: SUPPORT TEAM

Instant Gratitude

August 23

I am grateful for my intuitive desire to travel and all the resources I receive from the Universe. Where do you need me to be, Great Spirit? Here I am.

❀

Dear Reader: Do individuals who care a lot about people and animals deserve to receive prosperity—money, love, attention—far above bare minimum survival? Let's practice welcoming greater prosperity so we may serve others from a place of plenty.

My thoughts:

_____
_____
_____
_____
_____

Additional key words: HIGHER POWER and UNIVERSE / SERVICE / PROSPERITY and ABUNDANCE

August 24

I am grateful for strong but soft toilet paper. That's it. I am easy.

My thoughts:

_____
_____
_____
_____
_____

Additional key words: PROSPERITY and ABUNDANCE

Instant Gratitude

August 25

I am grateful I choose joy and hope over self-deprivation and judgment. There's a new twinkle in my eye, and I think I'll wear it every day.

My thoughts:

_____
_____
_____
_____
_____

Additional key words: PROSPERITY and ABUNDANCE / SPIRIT and SOUL

August 26

I am grateful to celebrate the happiness of loved ones in the birth of their babies, moving into new homes, and other blessed milestones.

My thoughts:

_____
_____
_____
_____
_____

Additional key words: FAMILY, VICTORY and CELEBRATION

Instant Gratitude

August 27

I am grateful for teenagers who approached me while I was lying on the grass. "Are you ok?" they asked. "Oh, I am relaxing, thanks." They gleefully shouted out to their friends, "She's alive!" Such *sweetness on earth*.

My thoughts:

_____

_____

_____

_____

_____

Additional key words: REST and RELAXATION / FUN / NATURE

August 28

I am grateful the Universe gives me lessons in small doses, although "small" sometimes feels like a hippopotamus. Thank goodness for an understanding Spirit I need not fully understand.

My thoughts:

_____
_____
_____
_____
_____

Additional key words: HIGHER POWER and UNIVERSE

Instant Gratitude

August 29

I am grateful for reminders to *live and let live* so that I do not compulsively throw too many rocks into my backpack.

❊

Dear Reader: What are you doing for yourself today that will bring you joy and laughter? Let's get good rest and food today to face the world feeling nourished.

My thoughts:

___
___
___
___
___

Additional key words: HEALTHY BOUNDARIES

August 30

I am grateful to realize that allowing wisdom, money and love to flow into my life stimulates prosperous energy. Receiving makes giving more possible.

My thoughts:

_____
_____
_____
_____
_____

Additional key words: MONEY / PROSPERITY /MINDSET

Instant Gratitude

August 31

I am grateful for air conditioning, especially in cars. Whenever I think about pioneers traveling across the country, I cannot imagine how they did it without air-conditioned horses.

My thoughts:

_____
_____
_____
_____
_____

Additional key words: PROSPERITY and ABUNDANCE

September 1

I am grateful for my healthy relationship with time. I set aside my ego and dial into what the Universe deems as a priority for the moment. *That* is my next right action.

My thoughts:

_____
_____
_____
_____
_____

Additional key words: TIME / HIGHER POWER and UNIVERSE

Instant Gratitude

September 2

I am grateful I can see there's room for improvement in my detaching from other people's drama. Life is far more beautiful when I make progress in this direction. *Amen!*

❈

Dear Reader: Can you remember a time when you set a firm boundary with determination to protect your sanity? Let's renew our commitment to staying centered and vibrant through any storm.

My thoughts:

_____
_____
_____
_____
_____

Additional key words: FAMILY / HEALTHY BOUNDARIES

September 3

I am grateful for the glow of sunsets upon the ocean—no fog, no clouds, just the sun melting into glistening water.

My thoughts:

_____
_____
_____
_____
_____

Additional key words: NATURE and WEATHER

Instant Gratitude

September 4

I am grateful to see how perfect each moment is even when adult stuff and responsibilities await my attention.

My thoughts:

_____
_____
_____
_____
_____

Additional key words: SPIRIT and SOUL

September 5

I am grateful for the Boston Red Sox's stamina and courage. Their winning a 7-hour, 19-inning game in 2015 continues to inspire me to envision victory and celebrate my mini- and mega-accomplishments. Thank God, *GO SOX,* and bless me!

My thoughts:

_____
_____
_____
_____
_____

Additional key words: SPORTS and ATHLETICS

Instant Gratitude

September 6

I am grateful for my really hip and cool text-aholic 60+ year-old mentor. I no longer need to settle for "LOL" when I can "LMAO." May you find something that makes you Laugh Your Ass Off today!

My thoughts:

_____
_____
_____
_____
_____

Additional key words: SUPPORT TEAM / FUN and LAUGHTER

September 7

I am grateful to find inspiration all over the place—reasons to celebrate, explore, collaborate, start, finish, laugh, share, and more. When I search for them, I find them. *Yay!*

My thoughts:

_____
_____
_____
_____
_____

Additional key words: INSPIRATION and CREATIVITY

Instant Gratitude

September 8

I am grateful to be able to let go of thoughts, things, and theories that are not working well for me. Goodbye, extra weight; hello, Light!

My thoughts:

_____

_____

_____

_____

_____

Additional key words: MINDSET / BODY / SELF CARE

September 9

I am grateful my higher power understands me so well, especially when I complicate things that could be made simple and confuse myself until tomorrow!

My thoughts:

_____
_____
_____
_____
_____

Additional key words: HIGHER POWER and UNIVERSE

Instant Gratitude

September 10

I am grateful that clarity around time and money yields truth about my levels of commitment in my relationships with self, Source, and others. Woohoo! This consistent flow of energy transforms creative visions into prosperous realities.

My thoughts:

_____
_____
_____
_____
_____

Additional key words: PROSPERITY and ABUNDANCE / TIME / MONEY

September 11

I am grateful to accept that catastrophes *will* happen. My job is to continue nourishing my spirit, body, mind, and heart so that I may offer something lovely to anyone the Universe brings into my life.

My thoughts:

_____
_____
_____
_____
_____

Additional key words: SPIRIT and SOUL

Instant Gratitude

September 12

I am grateful for inspiration to come out of my cave. Exploring, expanding, and connecting is just as important as meditating, writing, and resting.

❈

Dear Reader: When was the last time you thanked yourself for having the courage to leave your pajamas at home? Let's dissolve our fears and focus on offering something beautiful to the world in a way we've never done before!

My thoughts:

_____
_____
_____
_____
_____

Additional key words: SPIRIT and SOUL.

September 13

I am grateful for "coincidences" in my daily life. Frankly, I think it's the Universe giving me what I need *when I actually need it*. This serves the greater good, because we are connected as one.

My thoughts:

_____
_____
_____
_____
_____

Additional key words: HIGHER POWER and UNIVERSE / SERVICE

Instant Gratitude

September 14

I am grateful that connecting with my Creator throughout the day ignites out-of-the-box thinking and fuels me with courage to do things differently!

My thoughts:

_____

_____

_____

_____

_____

Additional key words: COURAGE and ACTION / HIGHER POWER and UNIVERSE

September 15

I am grateful for free car washes. All this rain has kept my white rocket ship looking quite respectable these days.

My thoughts:

_____
_____
_____
_____
_____

Additional key words: PROSPERITY and ABUNDANCE

Instant Gratitude

September 16

I am grateful for the beautiful habit of looking for and finding gratitude everywhere.

❁

Dear Reader: Might there be good but distracting thoughts in your mind that pull you from enjoying the present moment? Let's let go of those thoughts for the moment to make room for nourishing our precious hearts today.

My thoughts:

_____
_____
_____
_____
_____

Additional key words: SPIRIT and SOUL / MINDSET / BODY

September 17

I am grateful for people who earn a living making people laugh. Don't know what I'd do without them!

My thoughts:

_____
_____
_____
_____
_____

Additional key words: FUN and LAUGHTER

Instant Gratitude

September 18

I am grateful for doors that close so that I get to open new ones.

My thoughts:

_____
_____
_____
_____
_____

Additional key words: MINDSET

September 19

I am grateful that although I have an incredible number of major life projects on my plate, I still live as though everything is rigged in my favor. My angels have strong wings!

My thoughts:

___

___

___

___

___

Additional key words: UNIVERSE and HIGHER POWER, ABUNDANCE and PROSPERITY

Instant Gratitude

September 20

I am grateful to take actions that make sense in growing financial resources, like choosing to allow money to make money. Working smarter (not harder) is prosperity consciousness.

My thoughts:

_____
_____
_____
_____
_____

Additional key words: PROSPERITY and ABUNDANCE / MONEY

September 21

I am grateful for people in my life who are so patient with me when I cannot find words to express my feelings. Sometimes relaxing in a park or playing air hockey is the best that I can do. Making space for self is *serenity in action*.

My thoughts:

_____
_____
_____
_____
_____

Additional key words: SUPPORT TEAM / FUN

Instant Gratitude

September 22

I am grateful to be able to say that I no longer waste my time trying to convince anyone of anything. Accessing the serenity *within* me, I offer my thoughts with divine guidance.

My thoughts:

_____
_____
_____
_____
_____

Additional key words: SPIRIT and SOUL

September 23

I am grateful that my body is moving better and better in the morning, most likely because I am becoming healthier on the inside. Happy internal organs, happy life!

My thoughts:

_____
_____
_____
_____
_____

Additional key words: PROSPERITY and ABUNDANCE, BODY / INTERNAL ORGANS

Instant Gratitude

September 24

I am grateful for exclamation points!!!!! (x1,000) Happy Punctuation Day!

My thoughts:

_____
_____
_____
_____
_____

Additional key words: FUN and LAUGHTER / VICTORY and CELEBRATION

September 25

I am grateful for my lungs and all they do for me, even when I am not thinking about them, my right lung *and* my left one. I love you, my lungs!

My thoughts:

_____
_____
_____
_____
_____

Additional key words: BODY CARE / PROSPERITY and ABUNDANCE

Instant Gratitude

September 26

I am grateful for fresh air after a good rain. The blend of beautiful aromas awakens my senses and re-energizes my body.

My thoughts:

_____
_____
_____
_____
_____

Additional key words: NATURE and WEATHER

September 27

I am grateful for courage and persistence in finding solutions to problems faced by family and loved ones. Thank you, Great Spirit, for showing me the way.

❀

Dear Reader: What tools are helping you to make positive, energy-inviting decisions over impulsive, problem-creating ones? Let's use our tools every day to take good care of ourselves and loved ones *and* say "Yes!" to making wise investments in mental, physical, spiritual, and financial fitness.

My thoughts:

_____
_____
_____
_____
_____

Additional key words: FAMILY

Instant Gratitude

September 28

I am grateful to be pouring my heart into creating something that may bring relief to many. Although chaos historically repeats itself, I can nurture peace in the world in my very own way.

My thoughts:

_____
_____
_____
_____
_____

Additional key words: SPIRIT and SOUL / VICTORY and CELEBRATION

September 29

I am grateful for mornings in which I'm willing to align myself with my Creator, speak freely from my heart, and trust the Universe's timing in *everything*. Waking up with patience and serenity is so very sweet.

❀

Dear Reader: Can you recall a time that your day flowed more smoothly than you had expected? Let's recall the feeling of this magic throughout today and trust.

My thoughts:

_____
_____
_____
_____
_____

Additional key words: HIGHER POWER and UNIVERSE

Instant Gratitude

September 30

I am grateful to be able to design projects that have attainable goals. Reaching achievable milestones and crossing marathon finish lines feels fantastic!

My thoughts:

_____
_____
_____
_____
_____

Additional key words: VICTORY and CELEBRATION / PURPOSE

October 1

I am grateful that God guides me in scheduling my calendar and planning my days. What an awesome co-pilot!

My thoughts:
_____
_____
_____
_____
_____

Additional key words: TIME / HIGHER POWER and UNIVERSE

Instant Gratitude

October 2

I am grateful I am hopeful, hope-filled, and hope giving. For all the injustices I perceive in the world, this is a miracle. But for everything sad, there is something good whether or not I believe it. Universal law (polarity) and spiritual principles are timeless.

My thoughts:

_____
_____
_____
_____
_____

Additional key words: SPIRIT and SOUL.

October 3

I am grateful for my willingness to be still, not stuck in inertia but focused on moving energy within to restore flow and balance.

My thoughts:

Additional key words: SPIRIT and SOUL / BODY CARE

October 4

I am grateful to recognize fear, thank it for inspiring action, and replace it with faith that grows gardens.

❈

Dear Reader: Can you think of one fear that weighs heavily like a bag of rocks on your back? Let's write one fear or problem on a small piece of paper and put it in a box labeled "Universe."

My thoughts:

_____
_____
_____
_____
_____

Additional key words: MINDSET / COURAGE and ACTION / UNIVERSE and HIGHER POWER

October 5

I am grateful that when the Committee in my head says, "There is no solution," I pause, breathe, talk to God, reach out to someone, listen, breathe, make an attitude adjustment, and begin taking small actions toward vitality, visibility, and victory. The results? That's God's job.

My thoughts:

_____
_____
_____
_____
_____

Additional key words: UNIVERSE and HIGHER POWER / GOD / PROSPERITY and ABUNDANCE

Instant Gratitude

October 6

I am grateful for roasted root veggies—*yum*. Between just you and me, I'm so glad they are legal!

My thoughts:

_____
_____
_____
_____
_____

Additional key words: FOOD and NUTRIENTS

October 7

I am grateful that *every moment* is a chance for a fresh start. May I seize these gifts with gusto!

My thoughts:

Additional key words: MINDSET

October 8

I am grateful I allow myself to do things imperfectly. It right-sizes my ego and opens opportunities for joy.

My thoughts:

Additional key words: MINDSET

October 9

I am grateful I am willing to wear my grown-up pants—sometimes. *Just not today!*

❁

Dear Reader: In what ways can you make taking care of adult duties or responsibilities more fun today? Let's execute one task at a time with a bit of humor, wherever appropriate.

My thoughts:

_____
_____
_____
_____
_____

Additional key words: CHILD-LIKE JOY / FUN and LAUGHTER

Instant Gratitude

October 10

I am grateful for ten minutes of sunshine. This luxurious blanket heals me in ways that nothing else can.

My thoughts:

_____
_____
_____
_____
_____

Additional key words: NATURE and WEATHER

October 11

I am grateful that my Creator's ideas for me are so much better than my own. Incredibly insightful, multi-talented, and Spirit-loving people continue to waltz into my world. Good job, God!

My thoughts:

_____
_____
_____
_____
_____

Additional key words: HIGHER POWER and UNIVERSE / SUPPORT TEAM

Instant Gratitude

October 12

I am grateful for the chance to witness my mother's compassion for others in the Emergency Room. She touches people's hearts even though she is in pain.

My thoughts:

_____
_____
_____
_____
_____

Additional key words: FAMILY / LOVE / PAIN

October 13

I am grateful that monotasking is a very high priority for me. Staying focused on one thing at a time has improved my brain function, relaxed my nervous system (less pain), and allowed me to give myself fully to the person to whom I am speaking.

My thoughts:

_____
_____
_____
_____
_____

Additional key words: SPIRIT and SOUL / COURAGE and ACTION / PAIN

Instant Gratitude

October 14

I am grateful I give myself permission to relax my brain. When it gets too busy, we are all in trouble!

※

Dear Reader: What fond memories can you go to sleep with and wake up feeling refreshed? Let's replace "To Do" lists with loving thoughts at bedtime tonight.

My thoughts:

_____
_____
_____
_____
_____

Additional key words: SLEEP and REST

October 15

I am grateful I give myself permission to be a playful kid who is mindful of adult stuff, too. Blessings to the angels who carry me!

My thoughts:

_____
_____
_____
_____
_____

Additional key words: CHILD-LIKE JOY

Instant Gratitude

October 16

I am grateful I cherish who I am and not what I do. Enjoying being me inspires actions that create even more joy.

❈

Dear Reader: Do you have a favorite quote from a book, movie, or TED talk that inspires you to enjoy life to the fullest? Let's continue seeking thoughts to giggle and laugh about and then share them with others.

My thoughts:

_____
_____
_____
_____
_____

Additional key words: MINDSET / LAUGHTER / FUN

October 17

I am grateful for psychiatrists who see light in their patients' eyes and never give up on bringing them back to life.

My thoughts:

_____
_____
_____
_____
_____

Additional key words: SPIRIT and SOUL

Instant Gratitude

October 18

I am grateful for having let go of the angry person I used to be. The world is a better place when I am not high on judgment, outrage, or defiance. The love in my veins feels great!

My thoughts:

_____
_____
_____
_____
_____

Additional key words: MINDSET or LOVE

October 19

I am grateful to be fully aware of my limitations and to celebrate my progress *at the same time*!

My thoughts:

_____
_____
_____
_____
_____

Additional key words: HEALTH AND SAFETY / MINDSET / VICTORY and CELEBRATION

Instant Gratitude

October 20

I am grateful it is not necessary for me to know everything. There is only so much space in my head. When I am willing to ask the Universe for solutions, it shows me what I need and *when*.

My thoughts:

_____
_____
_____
_____
_____

Additional key words: HIGHER POWER and UNIVERSE

October 21

I am grateful for ideas different than my own. I am not the center of the Universe and do not know everything. Hard to believe, but true.

My thoughts:

_____
_____
_____
_____
_____

Additional key words: MINDSET

Instant Gratitude

October 22

I am grateful to be able to experience great excitement without losing focus on priorities and to ride through disappointment without going nuts. Stability rocks!

❁

Dear Reader: What little things could you do each day to keep your immune system strong and your emotional life stable? Let's write a list of gentle yet effective self-care activities to reach for when we are too tired to think.

My thoughts:

_____
_____
_____
_____
_____

Additional key words: MINDSET / VICTORY and CELEBRATION

October 23

I am grateful that when feeling *stuck*, I breathe deeply, stretch my body, and drink water!

My thoughts:

_____
_____
_____
_____
_____

Additional key words: BODY CARE

Instant Gratitude

October 24

I am grateful to see the connection between a loved one's excessive drinking, shopping, or gambling, and my drive to eat, hide, and take care of everyone but me. Detaching with love means I give myself space to breathe and time to celebrate my being.

My thoughts:

_____
_____
_____
_____
_____

Additional key words: HEALTHY BOUNDARIES

October 25

I am grateful that freedom is a matter of perception. We can gain all kinds and levels of freedom anywhere. Sometimes I need to work a bit harder to see it, but it *is* there!

My thoughts:

_____
_____
_____
_____
_____

Additional key words: MINDSET

Instant Gratitude

October 26

I am grateful to see signs that I am taking better care of my spirit. No longer spending time thinking about how wrong someone is about something, I can enjoy the Heaven in between my ears.

My thoughts:

_____

_____

_____

_____

_____

Additional key words: MINDSET / SPIRIT and SOUL.

October 27

I am grateful for Big Papi (David Ortiz), a true role model in my book. He is a self-care vigilante at 40 and will continue to share his talents and wisdom with countless generations.

❀

Dear Reader: Who comes to your mind, right now, as someone who *wows* you and inspires you to live life fully? Let's practice something today that we have learned from our healthy role models.

My thoughts:

_____
_____
_____
_____
_____

Additional key words: SPORTS and ATHLETICS / ROLE MODELS

Instant Gratitude

October 28

I am grateful that together we can celebrate opportunities for growth and laughter, despite the ups and downs of everyday life.

My thoughts:

_____
_____
_____
_____
_____

Additional key words: VICTORY and CELEBRATION

October 29

I am grateful for opportunities to interact with athletes and neuroscientists in the same room. I am living proof that neuroplasticity is not just another beautiful scientific theory; it's *my reality.*

My thoughts:

_____
_____
_____
_____
_____

Additional key words: SPORTS and ATHLETICS / BODY CARE

October 30

I am grateful my light bulb finally came on. What I "want" is overrated, because getting what I truly need turns out *even better* than fantasy. Who would've thunk?!?

My thoughts:

_____
_____
_____
_____
_____

Additional key words: SPIRIT and SOUL

October 31

I am grateful that a loved one's challenging behavior can inspire me to address *my own* fears around people, money, failure, *and* success.

❀

Dear Reader: Can you think of one person who would be happy for your success and one who might not be comfortable with it? Let's acknowledge both our confidence and insecurities and move forward with self-compassion all day long.

My thoughts:

_____
_____
_____
_____
_____

Additional key words: HEALTHY BOUNDARIES

Instant Gratitude

November 1

I am grateful to have made it through another demanding day; scheduled fun and relaxation time carried me across the finish line. Yay!

My thoughts:

_____
_____
_____
_____
_____

Additional key words: FUN and LAUGHTER / TIME / VICTORY and CELEBRATION

November 2

I am grateful for the experience of being a valuable connector between endless sky and earth. Alone in the middle of nowhere, I was at *the* center of everywhere. Blessings to the Hopi Reservation and Nation.

My thoughts:

_____
_____
_____
_____
_____

Additional key words: SPIRIT / SOUL

Instant Gratitude

November 3

I am grateful to discover more things to appreciate about myself. My Creator's plans for me to offer love and support to others require that I live in my positive attributes and talents.

My thoughts:

_____
_____
_____
_____
_____

Additional key words: SELF-WORTH / HIGHER POWER and UNIVERSE

November 4

I am grateful to have a group of friends with whom I spend time writing. We feel accomplished after every session. Yay!

My thoughts:

_____
_____
_____
_____
_____

Additional key words: SUPPORT TEAM / VICTORY and CELEBRATION

Instant Gratitude

November 5

I am grateful for alliances with survivors who live fully despite illness and pain. We are the faces of hope for those who suffer.

❃

Dear Reader: Can you think of one person whom you have allowed to help you or to whom you were kind? Let's offer smiles and "thank you's" to people we meet today and see what happens.

My thoughts:

_____
_____
_____
_____
_____

Additional key words: SUPPORT TEAM / PAIN

November 6

I am grateful that "Mondays" no longer haunt me, as I now see them as blessings. When I choose to stretch, pray, and play while doing adult things, all kinds of goodies appear!

My thoughts:

_____
_____
_____
_____
_____

Additional key words: BODY CARE / MINDSET

Instant Gratitude

November 7

I am grateful for nurturing affirmations. Thank goodness I can stop this noise, "I am not strong enough or deserving of good," and can replace it with "The old story is wrong. I am a treasure, and it is time I live like one!"

My thoughts:

_____
_____
_____
_____
_____

Additional key words: SELF-WORTH

November 8

I am grateful for this moment in which I am fine with everything as it is. At some point I might want to pout from the top of a mountain, but *not today*. Whew—thank you, God!

My thoughts:

_____
_____
_____
_____
_____

Additional key words: SPIRIT and SOUL / HIGHER POWER and UNIVERSE

Instant Gratitude

November 9

I am grateful for the beautiful bluebird that landed and walked around just a few feet away from my window while I was stretching this morning. I love you, little birdie!

My thoughts:

_____
_____
_____
_____
_____

Additional key words: NATURE and WEATHER

November 10

I am grateful for every bit of what I don't want to hear, because it eventually becomes useful when I least expect it.

My thoughts:

_____
_____
_____
_____
_____

Additional key words: MINDSET

Instant Gratitude

November 11

I am grateful for caring and alert medical professionals. Life is tough when they are sick. May all health care providers take the rest and good food they need to feel fantastic.

My thoughts:

_____
_____
_____
_____
_____

Additional key words: PUBLIC HEALTH and SAFETY / BODY / SELF-CARE

November 12

I am grateful for my desire and commitment to making this world a fun place so we may nourish our souls with everlasting fond memories!

❈

Dear Reader: What nice memories can you remember and feel grateful for at this very moment? Let's move forward in our day with wonderful feelings and energy!

My thoughts:

_____
_____
_____
_____
_____

Additional key words: SPIRIT and SOUL / FUN and LAUGHTER

Instant Gratitude

November 13

I am grateful for rare sunny winter mornings and my toasty ski jacket!

My thoughts:

_____
_____
_____
_____
_____

Additional key words: NATURE and WEATHER

November 14

I am grateful for many outstanding "light bulb moments." Once oblivious, I can now embrace wisdom, and make prosperous choices that before seemed unattainable. Universe has perfect timing!

My thoughts:

_____
_____
_____
_____
_____

Additional key words: MINDSET / HIGHER POWER and UNIVERSE

Instant Gratitude

November 15

I am grateful for time spent with wild turkeys while meditating in the sunshine. My heart grew more gentle and loving toward them, myself, and the world.

My thoughts:

_____
_____
_____
_____
_____

Additional key words: SPIRIT and SOUL / NATURE and WEATHER

November 16

I am grateful that when my mind is out to lunch, my gut takes the lead and guides me to places my mind never could have imagined.

My thoughts:

_____
_____
_____
_____
_____

Additional key words: MINDSET / WISDOM and INTUITION

Instant Gratitude

November 17

I am grateful for the ability to let go of what I have forgotten. If the Universe really wants to me to know or share something, I trust it will inspire me to speak up—*when* the time is right.

My thoughts:

_____
_____
_____
_____
_____

Additional key words: HIGHER POWER and UNIVERSE

November 18

I am grateful to embrace the idea that there are no coincidences. My job is to remain open, ask the Universe what my lesson is, and take the action right in front of me.

❈

Dear Reader: Do you recall a time when something miserable produced *positive* results? Let's take three deep breaths and actively seek every possible "yummy" out of every "yuckie" situation.

My thoughts:

_____
_____
_____
_____
_____

Additional key words: HIGHER POWER and UNIVERSE / COURAGE and ACTION

Instant Gratitude

November 19

I am grateful to be able to ignore the phrase "Don't even try. You can't do it." I allow my inner rebel to emerge with defiance, "Well, tough buggers. I did it!" Thank you, Higher Power.

My thoughts:

_____
_____
_____
_____
_____

Additional key words: COURAGE and ACTION

November 20

I am grateful to realize I have much to explore, learn, practice, and embrace. The Universe shows me when and how to handle anything that is within my hula hoop.

My thoughts:

Additional key words: HEALTHY BOUNDARIES / HIGHER POWER and UNIVERSE

Instant Gratitude

November 21

I am grateful that just saying "thank you" out loud is a powerful prayer, acknowledging God's grace and generosity.

My thoughts:

_____
_____
_____
_____
_____

Additional key words: PRAYER and MEDITATION

November 22

I am grateful I can create opportunities to be alone and regain my center.

My thoughts:

_____
_____
_____
_____
_____

Additional key words: SPIRIT and SOUL

Instant Gratitude

November 23

I am grateful to be able to sleep deeply and feel completely restored in the morning. You are looking at the wealthiest person on this planet!

My thoughts:

_____
_____
_____
_____
_____

Additional key words: PROSPERITY and ABUNDANCE / BODY / SLEEP and REST

November 24

I am grateful that whenever I seek validation from others, I can *pause* and then shift my focus to treasuring my heart and spirit.

My thoughts:

_____
_____
_____
_____
_____

Additional key words: MINDSET / HEALTHY BOUNDARIES

Instant Gratitude

November 25

I am grateful for the support of other writers who share, with good humor, their challenges in getting started on a project, maintaining a consistent schedule, and crossing the final finish line. Whew!

My thoughts:

_____
_____
_____
_____
_____

Additional key words: SUPPORT TEAM

November 26

I am grateful that when life is chaotic, I can climb into my imaginary boat under a blanket of stars and float on calm waters.

My thoughts:

_____
_____
_____
_____
_____

Additional key words: REST and RELAXATION / NATURE and WEATHER

Instant Gratitude

November 27

I am grateful that although there are people who tell me I don't do enough for them, I offer the best I can. And *that is enough!*

My thoughts:

_____
_____
_____
_____
_____

Additional key words: HEALTHY BOUNDARIES

November 28

I am grateful for boundaries—practicing love for self and compassion for others at the very same time.

My thoughts:
_____
_____
_____
_____
_____

Additional key words: HEALTHY BOUNDARIES

Instant Gratitude

November 29

I am grateful to be able to see silver linings and advantages of visiting, staying in, and working in hospitals. Opportunities to transform frowns into smiles completely fill my heart!

My thoughts:

_____
_____
_____
_____
_____

Additional key words: PUBLIC HEALTH AND SAFETY / SELF CARE / MINDSET

November 30

I am grateful for mental clarity during moments of crisis. Woohoo! A source of wisdom and strength carries me through seemingly impossible situations.

My thoughts:

_____
_____
_____
_____
_____

Additional key words: MINDSET / HIGHER POWER and UNIVERSE / PUBLIC HEALTH AND SAFETY

Instant Gratitude

December 1

I am grateful for obvious nudges the Universe gives me throughout the day. Following its guidance in taking care of top priorities, I stay centered while going to the right place and doing the right thing *at the right time.*

My thoughts:
_____
_____
_____
_____
_____

Additional key words: SPIRIT and SOUL

December 2

I am grateful for divine guidance in letting me know when to speak and when to listen. *Exquisite noise pollution* (seemingly helpful information) is everywhere, but I stay dialed into my gut for serenity.

❦

Dear Reader: What sounds can you bring into your everyday life that can soothe your soul, invigorate your body, or ignite your creative energy? Let's allow anything that is "music to our ears" to support us through everything.

My thoughts:

_____
_____
_____
_____
_____

Additional key words: MINDSET / GUT INTUITION

Instant Gratitude

December 3

I am grateful for extremely demanding days. Witnessing insanity in other people's lives has elevated to me a higher level of consciousness. In seeing the forest from the trees, I can detach with love, a beautiful expression of self-compassion.

My thoughts:

_____
_____
_____
_____
_____

Additional key words: HEALTHY BOUNDARIES

December 4

I am grateful to admit that my conscious mind is a pain in the butt sometimes; however, I can choose to go with my gut. God really reaches me *there*. Hallelujah!

My thoughts:

_____
_____
_____
_____
_____

Additional key words: MINDSET / GUT INTUITION

Instant Gratitude

December 5

I am grateful that my passion for learning how to read and retrain my nervous system is aiding others in feeling fantastic. Our bodies will continue to reveal the truth, and we will never stop being amazed.

My thoughts:

_____
_____
_____
_____
_____

Additional key words: BODY CARE

December 6

I am grateful my pain no longer keeps me up through the night. As soon as my eyes are closed, peaceful sleep hugs me.

My thoughts:

_____
_____
_____
_____
_____

Additional key words: SLEEP and REST / PAIN

Instant Gratitude

December 7

I am grateful that even when life gets busy, I can take a moment to step out of it, address what is my responsibility, and leave the rest to others.

My thoughts:

_____
_____
_____
_____
_____

Additional key words: HEALTHY BOUNDARIES

December 8

I am grateful for reminders of how I used to look, feel, and struggle when I believed in my intellectual ability to manage my life. Today, my spirituality is practical: gut intuition overrides mental constipation, and I feel fantastic inside and out!

My thoughts:

_____
_____
_____
_____
_____

Additional key words: SPIRIT and SOUL / WISDOM and INTUITION

Instant Gratitude

December 9

I am grateful for clear, reasonable goals I can meet throughout the day; letting go of belongings and thoughts that no longer serve me, I feel lighter.

My thoughts:

_____
_____
_____
_____
_____

Additional key words: SPIRIT and SOUL / PURPOSE

December 10

I am grateful to have overheard a man talking to his goats while feeding them this morning. "No, not you. You've eaten already." Ahh, goats and I *do* have sooo much in common.

My thoughts:

_____
_____
_____
_____
_____

Additional key words: SPIRIT and SOUL

Instant Gratitude

December 11

I am grateful for willingness to explore new ways of seeing myself. This requires courage, but I have enough evidence showing there are undiscovered goodies hidden inside me. Okay, world, I am ready to climb, dig, or whatever!

My thoughts:

___

___

___

___

___

Additional key words: COURAGE and ACTION

December 12

I am grateful that the more I learn about my family history, the greater my appreciation for my health and sanity. It's a miracle we are still alive!

My thoughts:

_____
_____
_____
_____
_____

Additional key words: FAMILY

December 13

I am grateful that when people tell me I should buy this and that, go here and there, or work more and more, I can pause for wisdom from within my body or just say out loud, "Hi God, it's me calling!"

❈

Dear Reader: What difficult task do you need to do today that might go more smoothly with a flow of energy from a powerful source that moves planets? Let's tap into that energy today!

My thoughts:

_____
_____
_____
_____
_____

Additional key words: MINDSET / HIGHER POWER / HEALTHY BOUNDARIES

December 14

I am grateful for baby chicks, pandas, Santa Claus, the Easter Bunny, baseball, and fast cars. Adulthood has its privileges.

My thoughts:

_____
_____
_____
_____
_____

Additional key words: FUN and LAUGHTER

December 15

I am grateful for the time-planning strategy, "Subtract, not add." It is especially powerful during the holidays; setting aside extra time in between activities is precious time-care and compassionate self-care.

My thoughts:

_____
_____
_____
_____
_____

Additional key words: TIME

December 16

I am grateful for the expression, "Less is more"; it reminds me that when I do less "busy work," I make more time for meaningful experiences.

My thoughts:

Additional key words: TIME

Instant Gratitude

December 17

I am grateful that practicing self-care leads to more frequent moments of clarity. It is much easier to tackle difficulties *with the light on* than to stumble around wearing a veil of vagueness.

My thoughts:

_____
_____
_____
_____
_____

Additional key words: BODY CARE

December 18

I am grateful to realize that other people's separation anxiety and need to know where I am doesn't have to smother me. Ahh—how exhilarating it is to breathe freely!

My thoughts:

_____
_____
_____
_____
_____

Additional key words: HEALTHY BOUNDARIES

Instant Gratitude

December 19

I am grateful for reminders *not* to seek external validation. Everything I need is *within* me.

My thoughts:

_____
_____
_____
_____
_____

Additional key words: SPIRIT and SOUL

December 20

I am grateful to acknowledge that scheduling time to relax during the holidays can be tough. However, resting (and rehydrating) boosts my immune system and supports me in making healthy decisions about money, food, time, travel, and people!

❖

Dear Reader: Whom can you reach out to for motivation to stay in tune with your body today? Let's step out of our comfort zone with someone who would love to cheer us on!

My thoughts:

_____
_____
_____
_____
_____

Additional key words: SELF CARE and FOOD / IMMUNE HEALTH / PROSPERITY and ABUNDANCE

Instant Gratitude

December 21

I am grateful for meridian EFT tapping and chi gong, for they help me release stuck energy and rebalance its flow in my body. With serenity and confidence, I can better face the world's whirlwind of drama.

My thoughts:

_____
_____
_____
_____
_____

Additional key words: BODY CARE / SPIRIT and SOUL / HIGHER POWER

December 22

I am grateful noise pollution sometimes hijacks my head and reminds me to schedule rest and meditation. When I realign my thoughts and actions with my Creator, I kick butt!

My thoughts:

Additional key words: MINDSET / SLEEP and REST / HIGHER POWER and UNIVERSE

December 23

I am grateful to be able to pause before reacting to anything. To me, responding from a place of peace is one of the most self-compassionate acts.

My thoughts:

_____
_____
_____
_____
_____

Additional key words: MINDSET / SPIRIT and SOUL

December 24

I am grateful for my faith in God, Sweetness, and everything good. Darkness fades when light is bright.

My thoughts:

_____
_____
_____
_____
_____

Additional key words: HIGHER POWER and UNIVERSE

Instant Gratitude

December 25

I am grateful for the reminder that I can create new traditions for celebrating anything ANY day of the year. I embrace the party animal in me! Woohoo!

My thoughts:

_____
_____
_____
_____
_____

Additional key words: FUN AND LAUGHTER

December 26

I am grateful for courage to ask for what I think I want. Universe responds to me with a "Yes," "Not now," or "There is something *better* for you."

My thoughts:

_____
_____
_____
_____
_____

Additional key words: COURAGE and ACTION / PRAYER and MEDITATION / HIGHER POWER and UNIVERSE

Instant Gratitude

December 27

I am grateful to have a program of action so even when I am lacking motivation, I can still move forward each day. Depression, insecurity, and lack of hope do *not* stand a chance!

My thoughts:

_____
_____
_____
_____
_____

Additional key words: COURAGE and ACTION

December 28

I am grateful for my willingness to embrace focusing on one thing at a time. Monotasking is healthier for the nervous system than multitasking.

❖

Dear Reader: Can you think of a regular activity you do, like walking, driving, eating, or working, during which you find yourself pausing to fix mistakes from doing several things at once? Let's enjoy being more efficient by respecting the person right in front of us and the task at hand and save ourselves time, energy, and money!

My thoughts:

_____
_____
_____
_____
_____

Additional key words: TIME / MONEY / BODY CARE

Instant Gratitude

December 29

I am grateful that there are different ways to look at everything. I love having so many options!

My thoughts:

_____

_____

_____

_____

_____

Additional key words: MINDSET

December 30

I am grateful I've overcome my knee-jerk reaction to other people's drama. I discern when the Universe needs me to respond wisely.

My thoughts:

___

Additional key words: HEALTHY BOUNDARIES / HIGHER POWER and UNIVERSE

Instant Gratitude

December 31

I am grateful for my willingness to reflect on qualities I admire in others so that I can take bite-sized steps toward developing those yummy attributes in me!

My thoughts:

_____
_____
_____
_____
_____

Additional key words: MINDSET

Bonus Gratitude Expression #1:

I am grateful that no matter what life brings me, I stay in gratitude and pray for clarity. Every day is the first day of the rest of my life, filled with a higher quality of sobriety in my thoughts, feelings, and actions. I am glad to be here with you.

My thoughts:

_____
_____
_____
_____
_____

Additional key words: PRAYER and MEDITATION

Instant Gratitude

Bonus Gratitude Expression #2:

I am grateful for my personal advisory team. They sustain my light through moments of doubt and cheer me on to new heights!

My thoughts:

_____
_____
_____
_____
_____

Additional key words: SUPPORT TEAM

Bonus Gratitude Expression #3:

I am grateful that God does wonderful work while I sleep. What a fantastic co-pilot I have!

My thoughts:

_____
_____
_____
_____
_____

Additional key words: HIGHER POWER and UNIVERSE

Instant Gratitude

Bonus Gratitude Expression #4:

I am grateful I give myself permission to rest and take my mind off the world without abandoning it forever.

My thoughts:

_____
_____
_____
_____
_____

Additional key words: SLEEP and REST

Bonus Gratitude Expression #5:

I am grateful my gut pays attention to what is right before me, even when my head seems to be on another planet. Thank goodness for intuition!

My thoughts:

_____
_____
_____
_____
_____

Additional key words: WISDOM and INTUITION

Bonus Gratitude Expression #6:

I am grateful to have faced loneliness square in the eye. Being honest with myself helps me connect with loving people and makes life worth living. I am now complete.

My thoughts:

_____
_____
_____
_____
_____

Additional key words: SPIRIT and SOUL

Bonus Gratitude Expression #7:

I am grateful I finally realized just how much my happiness depended on others' willingness to be well. Now I am honoring my thirst for life and letting Source do its job.

My thoughts:

_____
_____
_____
_____
_____

Additional key words: HEALTHY BOUNDARIES

Bonus Gratitude Expression #8:

I am grateful for divine guidance in listening for what I need to hear and disengaging from what does not strengthen me. Making healthy choices *rocks*!

My thoughts:

_____
_____
_____
_____
_____

Additional key words: PRAYER and MEDITATION

Index

ATTITUDE: x, 60, 82, 85, 198, 278
BODY CARE (See "Self-Care"): 5, 9, 14, 22-23, 29, 34, 40, 44, 48, 51, 61, 68, 93-95, 97, 100, 104, 132, 136, 141, 146, 159, 166-167, 192, 196, 213, 219, 226, 228, 268, 276, 296, 302, 310, 339, 351, 355, 362
CELEBRATION and VICTORY: 6, 21, 77, 107, 114, 120, 144, 156, 158, 204, 220, 224, 229, 238, 248, 267, 271, 273, 292, 295, 301, 305, 308
CHILD-LIKE JOY: 19, 25, 43, 57, 70, 112, 124, 138, 198, 217, 225, 282, 288
CONFIDENCE (inner strength): 27, 31, 154, 304, 355
COURAGE and ACTION: 13, 39, 45, 60, 73, 119, 162, 197, 216, 257, 277, 286, 322-323, 345, 360-361
CREATIVITY and INSPIRATION: 20, 88, 110, 250
EFT (See "Emotional Freedom Technique" or "Tapping"): xi, 47, 355
EMOTIONAL FREEDOM TECHNIQUE (See "EFT" or "Tapping"): xi
FAMILY: 135, 167, 176, 199, 238, 245, 270, 285, 346
FOOD and NUTRIENTS (See "Self-Care/Body"): 4, 29, 34, 47, 54, 67, 96, 128, 135, 140, 157, 180, 191-192, 199, 229, 279
FUN and LAUGHTER (See "Self-Care/Mind"): 53, 66, 79-80, 82, 87, 101, 108, 133, 163-164, 166, 168, 173, 176, 179, 201, 215, 249, 260, 267, 282, 305, 316, 348, 359

GOALS (See "Mindset" and "Time"): 84, 273, 343

GOD: 8, 11, 27, 32, 47, 62, 72, 92, 99, 114, 129, 141, 178, 181, 184, 187, 199-200, 212, 248, 274, 278, 284, 312, 325, 338, 347, 358, 368

GREAT SPIRIT (See "God" or "Universe"): 8, 11, 69, 232, 235, 270

GUT INTUITION: xi, 28, 69, 77, 195, 226, 336, 338, 342

HEALTHY BOUNDARIES (See "Relationships"): xi, 32, 73, 188, 193, 241, 245, 297, 304, 324, 328, 331-332, 337, 341, 347, 352, 364, 372

HIGHER POWER: xi, 8, 11-12, 21, 23-24, 41, 44, 47, 52, 56, 62, 65, 69, 92, 99, 105, 111, 123, 129, 131, 134, 137, 141, 153, 161, 170, 175, 178, 184, 187, 199, 205, 212, 216, 232, 235, 240, 244, 252, 256-257, 262, 272, 274, 277-278, 284, 293, 307, 312, 318, 321-324, 334, 347, 355-356, 358, 360, 364, 368

INSPIRATION and CREATIVITY: 20, 88, 110, 250

INTESTINES (See "Self-Care/Body"): 29, 34, 128, 132, 140

INTUITION: xi, 28, 69, 77, 152, 195, 218, 226, 320, 336, 338, 342, 370

LAUGHTER and FUN: 53, 66, 79-80, 82, 87, 101, 108, 133, 163-164, 166, 168, 173, 176, 179, 201, 215, 249, 260, 267, 282, 305, 316, 348, 359

LOVE: ix, x, xi, 22, 31, 34, 45, 74, 78, 124, 129, 138, 141, 156, 167, 179, 184, 209, 235, 242, 268, 285, 291, 297, 307, 313, 332, 337, 354, 363

MIND (See "Self-Care"): xi, 45, 77, 82, 106, 111, 152, 159-160, 171, 182, 193, 195, 254, 259, 300, 320, 338, 369

MINDSET: 10, 12, 16, 25, 35, 59, 61, 64, 71, 75-76, 85, 91, 95, 103, 105, 109, 117, 125, 132, 155, 158-160, 171, 185, 190, 195, 211, 214, 224, 233, 242, 251, 259, 261, 277, 280-281, 289, 291-292, 294-295, 298-299, 310, 314, 318, 320, 328, 333-334, 336, 338, 347, 356-357, 363, 365

MONEY: 69, 77, 112, 138, 235, 242, 253, 263, 304, 354, 362

NATURE and WEATHER: 11, 20, 63, 72, 76, 112, 115, 129-130, 138, 147, 189, 196, 208, 215, 219, 246, 269, 283, 313, 317, 319, 330

PAIN: xi, 33, 66, 122, 203, 285-286, 309, 338, 340

PEE (See "Self-Care/Immune System"): 30, 55, 225

POOP (See "Self-Care/Immune System"): 34, 55, 68, 132

PRAYER and MEDITATION: 15, 91, 99, 106, 113, 178, 203, 230, 325, 360, 366, 373

PROSPERITY and ABUNDANCE: xi, 1, 12, 33, 46, 52, 55, 58, 98, 116, 121, 145, 148-149, 165, 169, 186, 194, 200, 222, 235-237, 243, 253, 258, 263, 266, 268, 278, 327, 354

Instant Gratitude

PUBLIC HEALTH and SAFETY: 37, 48, 90, 167, 207, 315, 333-334

PURPOSE: 2, 13, 84, 88, 273, 343

RELATIONSHIPS (See "Healthy Boundaries"): 156, 253

ROLE MODELS (See "Support Team"): 17, 88, 93, 122, 151, 204, 227, 300

SELF-CARE: ix, x, xi, xii, 14, 23, 25-26, 30, 51, 77, 90, 104, 146, 149, 156, 174, 193, 221, 295, 300, 315, 349, 351

   BODY: xi, 1, 4-5, 9, 14, 22-23, 29-30, 33-34, 40, 44, 48, 51, 54, 61-62, 66-68, 77, 82, 89, 93-95, 97, 100, 103-104, 111, 116, 123, 126, 128, 132, 136, 141, 146, 150, 159, 166-167, 182, 191-193, 196, 209, 213, 219, 226, 228, 251, 254, 259, 266, 268-269, 276, 296, 302, 310, 315, 327, 336, 339, 347, 351, 354-355, 362

   - Immune System/Intestines/Organs: 5, 29, 34, 51, 128, 132, 140, 171, 295, 354

   - Circulatory System/Heart/Movement: 2, 45, 100, 115, 149, 161-162, 171, 203, 254, 271-272, 319, 328, 333

   HABITS (body, mind, spirit): 6, 48, 51, 185, 207

   - Exercise (breathing and stretching): 23, 34, 72, 89, 95, 97, 112, 114, 116, 132, 141, 159, 162, 192, 204, 219, 228, 296, 310, 313, 377, 382

   - Food and Nutrients: 4, 29, 34, 47, 54, 67, 96, 128, 135, 140, 157, 180, 191-192, 199, 229, 279

   - Laughter: ix, x, 17, 52-53, 61, 66, 79-80, 82, 87, 98, 101, 108, 122, 127, 133, 144, 163-164, 166, 168, 173, 176, 179, 201, 215, 225, 241, 249, 260, 267, 282, 289, 301, 305, 316, 348, 359

   - Prayer and Meditation: 15, 91, 99, 106, 113, 178, 203, 230, 325, 360, 366, 373

   - Sleep and Rest: 31, 50, 111-112, 138, 174, 206, 221, 230, 287, 327, 340, 356, 369

   MIND (See "MINDSET"): xi, 45, 77, 82, 106, 111, 152, 159-160, 171, 182, 193, 195, 254, 259, 300, 320, 338, 369

   - Brain / Neuroplasticity: ix, x, xi, 28, 69, 91, 128, 158, 160, 195-196, 286-287, 302

      Compulsion and Depression: xi, 82, 181, 361, 209

   SPIRIT (See "SPIRIT and SOUL")

   - Child-like joy: 19, 25, 43, 57, 70, 112, 124, 138, 198, 217, 225, 282, 288

- Laughter: ix, x, 17, 52-53, 61, 66, 79-80, 82, 87, 98, 101, 108, 122, 127, 133, 144, 163-164, 166, 168, 173, 176, 179, 201, 215, 225, 241, 249, 260, 267, 282, 289, 301, 305, 316, 348, 359
- Meditation: x, 15, 91, 93, 99, 106, 113, 178, 203, 230, 325, 356, 360, 366, 373
- Prayer: 15, 74, 91, 99, 106, 113, 178, 203, 230, 325, 360, 366, 373
- Wisdom: x, 28, 42, 44, 60, 62, 69, 119, 152, 195, 218, 226, 232, 242, 300, 318, 320, 334, 342, 347, 370

SELF-WORTH: 1, 10, 26, 78, 123, 144, 173, 175, 184, 187, 307, 311

SERENITY: xi, 2, 30, 32-33, 43, 76, 106, 117, 224, 264-265, 272, 336, 355

SERVICE: 26, 37, 186, 235, 256

SLEEP and REST (See "Self-Care/Body" and "Self-Care/Mind"): 31, 50, 111-112, 138, 174, 206, 221, 230, 287, 327, 340, 356, 369

SOBRIETY: xi, 77, 177, 366

SOURCE: xi, 8, 11, 44, 110, 253, 334, 347, 372

SPIRIT and SOUL (See "Self-Care"): 7, 16, 18, 23, 27, 32, 42-43, 45, 47, 49, 56, 59, 63, 74, 78, 81-82, 86-87, 92, 94, 102, 117, 122, 137, 139, 142-143, 146, 172, 177, 181-183, 185, 190, 200, 202-204, 210, 223, 232, 237, 247, 254-255, 259, 265, 271, 275-276, 286, 290, 299, 303, 312, 316, 319, 326, 335, 342-344, 353, 355, 357, 371

SPORTS and ATHLETICS: 22, 41, 89, 248, 300, 302

SUCCESS: 87, 114, 144, 304

SUPPORT TEAM (See "Role Models"): 3, 17, 36, 38, 46, 58, 65, 81, 83-84, 118-119, 127, 129, 133, 147, 154, 174, 176, 179, 205, 227, 234, 249, 264, 284, 308-309, 329, 367

TAPPING (See "EFT" or "Emotional Freedom Technique"): xi, 34, 47, 97, 355

TIME: xi, 15, 24, 30, 63, 69, 73, 84, 89, 92, 100, 109, 125, 127, 129, 152-153, 162, 166, 172, 174, 182, 185, 191, 202, 212-213, 221, 223, 227, 230, 244-245, 253, 255, 265, 272, 274, 282, 286, 292, 297, 299, 305, 308, 311, 319, 321-322, 332, 335, 349-350, 354, 362

UNIVERSE: x, xi, xii, 2-3, 8, 11-12, 21, 23, 27, 41, 44, 47, 52, 56, 62, 65, 69, 88, 92, 98-99, 105, 111, 116, 129, 134, 137, 141, 153, 161, 170, 175, 178, 184, 187, 196, 199, 205, 212, 216, 227, 232, 235, 240, 244, 252, 254, 256-257, 262, 272, 274, 277-278, 284, 293-294, 307, 312, 318, 321-322,

324, 334-335, 356, 358, 360, 364, 368

VICTORY and CELEBRATION: 6, 21, 77, 107, 114, 120, 132, 144, 156, 158, 204, 220, 224, 229, 238, 248, 267, 271, 273, 292, 295, 301, 305, 308

WEATHER and NATURE: 11, 20, 63, 72, 76, 112, 115, 129-130, 131, 138, 147, 189, 196, 208, 215, 219, 231, 239, 246, 269, 283, 313, 317, 319, 330

WORK: 2, 7, 347, 350, 368

Acknowledgements

In 2013, a small group of friends said "yes" to my offering to text them one item on my gratitude list each morning so they could jumpstart their day with one of mine and begin a list of their own. Thanks to them, I have enjoyed years of receiving text messages filled with their expressions of gratitude, photos, and funny stories throughout the day, every single day. Letting people know I remember them daily has created a rich life, filled with people offering me joy as well.

I have learned that when the Universe deems something as a priority, responding positively is a good idea. In 2017, three individuals who had never met each other asked me to publish these gratitude text blasts in a book. After much coaxing, I publicly announced my commitment to this project, and here we are after long hours of giggles and laughs, interspersed with vigilant self-care—deep breathing, stretching, tapping, chi gong, walking along the river, yoga, rehydrating, eating gourmet meals, spending time with family and friends, and always connecting with a powerful source of wisdom, courage, and humor.

I wish to acknowledge and thank my team of editors and artistic muses: Lynn Kennedy Baxter, Giovanni Dortch, Mica Vincent, Elizabeth Vitale, and Elana Kundell. Last, but not least, I am very grateful for my daughter Nadya and her casual yet profound influence on the overall look and feel of this book. She made perfect suggestions right when I needed them. We seek; the Universe delivers.

About Ilana Kristeva

Ilana Kristeva, M.P.A., is the "Self-Care Vigilante," an out-of-the-box proponent of self-care practices that honor profound wisdom from a wide spectrum of healing modalities—West to East and new to ancient. An author, speaker, and Vibrance Coach, Ilana promotes public awareness of health and safety issues through her books, audio books, and public appearances demonstrating Pro EFT "tapping" and Chi Gong. Most importantly, this inspirational speaker manages her chronic systemic disease—Complex Regional Pain Syndrome (CRPS)—and other serious health conditions with grace, ease, and laughter. In her spare time, Ilana performs Self-Care Comedy™ and coaches the Boston Red Sox from the middle of her living room floor.

In addition to *Instant Gratitude: 365 Days of Grace, Ease, and Laughter*, Ilana Kristeva is the author of *Birth of a Self-Care Vigilante, Tap into the Universe for Recovery, Book 1*.

Made in the USA
Columbia, SC
28 June 2023